THE

MASTER

OF

LUCID DREAMS

Also by Olga Kharitidi, M.D.

Entering the Circle:
The Secrets of Ancient Siberian Wisdom
Discovered by a Russian Psychiatrist

the MASTER OF LUCID DREAMS

OLGA KHARITIDI, M.D.

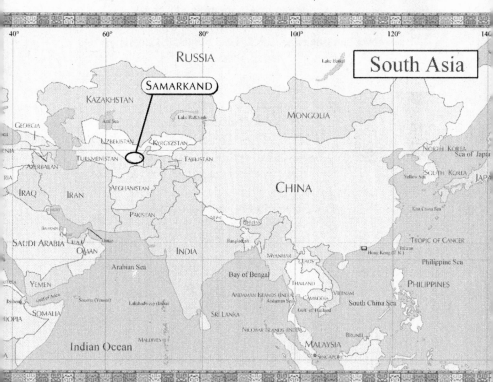

HAMPTON ROADS
PUBLISHING COMPANY, INC.

for the evolving human spirit

Cover design by Marjoram Productions
Cover photo by Daniel C. Waugh
Back cover and title page map © 1993 Magellan Geographix (sm),
Santa Barbara, CA

Hampton Roads Publishing Company, Inc.
Charlottesville, VA 22906
www.hrpub.com

Library of Congress Catalog Card Number: 2001094009
ISBN 978-1-57174-329-9

Printed on acid-free paper in Canada
TCP
10 9 8 7 6 5 4

Prologue

I didn't have any expectations. I was just sitting there, looking at the fire, which soon became the focus of my vision. Only Sulema's face on another side of the fire was still visible to me. I heard her saying, "We love storytelling here. Can you tell me a story now? Tell me the most puzzling story you know." I thought Sulema asked me that just to help me feel comfortable, and I was grateful to her for that.

"Now?"

"Sure, why not?"

I thought about her suggestion for a while, and then suddenly the story of Hamlet, a story that had been puzzling me since high school, came suddenly to my mind.

"All right, I know such a story. It has been puzzling me for years since I never was able to find any final, complete, and unambiguous meaning to it. This story happened long ago.

"There was a prince who lived in a faraway land. His father had died recently. His mother married his uncle and the uncle became the king, and the prince lived in his kingdom. He wasn't a particularly sad prince and he wasn't particularly lonely. He definitely wasn't mad, until one day when everything changed and the prince began to change.

"That day, or more exactly that night, he met the ghost of his dead father, who told him a story of how the reigning king, his own brother, poisoned him to death to get the kingdom and the queen. His father's ghost demanded revenge, and there was no more peace left for the prince after he learned that story.

"He invented a clever trick: he invited wandering actors to perform for the king and the queen with a play the prince created himself. The play was the story of his father's murder, played out by actors before the prince's mother and his uncle. He saw the proof of guilt in their faces as they watched the play, and then he became truly mad."

"He was killed, right? The prince is killed at the end of the story, right?" Sulema interrupted me without waiting for me to finish.

"Actually yes, he was. You know the story?"

"That ghost killed him, the ghost of his father."

"Actually, no . . ."

"Actually, yes. He started to play by the rules of the ghost. He let the spirit of trauma in, into himself; he allowed the demon to invade his memory with the hurt of his father's death and to become a part of himself. He started acting from the spirit's command, so he had to be killed. He didn't become mad, as you say. He was just fighting the spirit of trauma. He lost, I guess. He didn't have any wife, did he?"

"No. But he had a fiancée with whom he was very tender at first, but then she killed herself because of his rudeness and madness."

"Whoa! Were there more dead people in this story?"

"Actually, yes. The bride's father and . . ."

"Oh! A really hungry ghost he was, that father look-alike. That was a good story. The one who wrote it knew about the battle."

Sulema grew silent and her squinting eyes looked straight at me through the fire as if she was seeing through me. I saw her kind smile through the flames until they rose up again and her face became hidden behind the fire.

I started to feel how my bodily sensations changed. It felt as if some invisible power penetrated my tensed muscles and untied the old painful knots stored in them. Along with that, I felt my memory was liberating and changing itself into the same substance of which dreams are made, and soon a stream of images was flowing through my mind. They flowed in abundance, but there was no chaos to it; they were all connected by an invisible, profound order and my perception followed this.

The fire kept moving slightly, but its shape now was perfectly round as if the sun, by a miracle, were burning in front of me in a duplicate of itself. I stared at it for a while, until everything turned red, and the sun disk became black. I closed my eyes and felt how this little sun in front of me was pulsating and approaching me. I tried to stay still, very, very still, until I heard the noise, like a gate opening, and Michael's voice said:

"Fear nothing and remember that it is the Father who punishes and it is the Mother who forgives. I will be with you when you need me."

Chapter I

I suddenly awakened. In the narrow hospital bed, my body recognized in a moment the jump my awareness made as it shifted itself away from sleep. My mind was more resistant, though, to leaving a dream so quickly. It stayed confused for a while, trying to decide whether the alarm that pulled me out of the dream was a woman's cry, still sounding in my ears, or something else.

It was a phone call. The woman's cry was the last remnant of my dream, and it faded quickly, evading my attempts to catch it. And when I answered the phone, the dream disappeared completely, leaving the anxiety pressed against my heart as the only memory of it.

I looked at my watch. It was 2:30 A.M. I was being called for an emergency psychiatric evaluation in the main hospital. That meant forgetting about sleep for the rest of my on-call night.

I had to run through the hospital grounds, my way lit by indifferent stars shining distantly above in the wintry night sky. The Siberian State Hospital was one of the largest in Novosibirsk, with a thousand patients remaining there for months and sometimes for years. It was built a distance from the city, near the forest and far away from homes. The security was quite good there, and to escape the ward was almost as difficult as escaping from a Soviet prison.

Still, the hospital was surrounded by an aura of danger and mystery for neighboring people, and once in a while a group of boys would show up on the grounds daring themselves to get closer to the building's walls and to look inside behind the grated windows. At night the hospital grounds were empty, and darkness surrounded them on all sides. I tried to cross the distance between my warm on-call room and the emergency quarter of the main hospital as quickly as I could. I was wearing only a white gown and no overcoat and trying to beat the freeze of the night by getting to the ER before the cold could reach me.

I heard her screaming even before I opened the massive ice-covered iron back door to the ER. Her cry hit my ears at the same moment I reached the door, and all the cold accumulated in its metal handle set fire to my bare hand.

"Let me go! I tell you, let me go!" she was screaming loudly. The minute I entered the warm corridor, I saw her restrained with wide, black leather bandages, fixed to a hard stretcher, banging her head from side to side. Two new ER orderlies obviously hadn't had much experience with psychiatric patients and, trying to look professionally distant, they rushed the stretcher and patient through the empty hospital corridor to transfer her to me as soon as possible.

I had to walk in long strides behind them to keep up with their pace. This nighttime run through ER corridors, lit to look like day, was waking me up quickly. When the orderlies made a last turn and entered the examination room, I was completely shaken out of my too-short on-call sleep.

"Thank you. You may untie her now and wait for me outside." My voice still sounded a little harsh from sleep, but my mind had already been restored to its professional alertness.

The orderlies looked at me with traces of doubt. I just gave a firm nod, showing them that I knew what I was doing. The patient didn't look psychotic despite her extreme agitation. I knew that the presence of these two men wouldn't do me any good, but would more likely interfere with the quality of my interview instead. They quickly untied the bandages, which had already left hurting marks on her thin wrists, and vanished obediently from the room.

"My name is Dr. Kharitidi. I am a psychiatrist at the hospital. I was called for your evaluation."

The woman, now surprisingly calm, was slowly trying to sit up on the stretcher. I came to her and helped her let her legs down, covering them with a white flannel sheet; the number eight ink-stamped on its corner indicated the ward. She was obviously drowsy. I looked quickly through her papers: thirty-nine years old, unmarried, suicide attempt with medication overdose. According to an ER physician, she was unresponsive when her neighbor brought her to the hospital. The ER stabilized her medically, and it was my job now to decide what to do next.

"What is your name, please?"

The woman looked at me for the first time. Her wildly disheveled black hair flared around her thin face. She slowly pulled it back as if wanting to tie it up, but then her hands fell weakly down to her knees. She was obviously exhausted by all her movements.

"Katherine," she answered in a whisper. Her scream a few moments ago seemed to have drained the last of her energy.

"I need to ask you a few questions, Katherine."

She slowly nodded her head in agreement.

I sat down in front of her on a metal chair placed near the sink, the only furniture in this little square room.

"Can you please tell me why you tried to hurt yourself?"

"It was an accident," she said slowly and looked away, breathing heavily.

I looked at her for some time and could clearly see the struggle which was going on inside her—between the desire to relieve her pain by talking to anybody, and the extreme shame from thinking that her humiliation would become known.

"I know that it wasn't an accident. I know that you tried to kill yourself tonight and I know that you came pretty close to succeeding. The real accident was that your neighbor found you before it was all over. I don't see any reason for you to be afraid of talking about it now. You had the strength to overcome the fear of dying. What can you possibly be afraid of now?"

She lifted her head and looked at me with concentration. Her eyes were full of extreme pain. I saw how my suggestion was liberating something inside her. My next professional task would be to become ready to handle this liberation.

"That's true. I wanted to die. No. I want to die. I only wish this thought had come to me earlier, many years earlier, to spare me from all the time I have wasted with my worthless life." She was more angry than sad, and her voice was rising higher while she was talking.

"I know that as soon as I crush this body, I will end the rest of it too. I will stop this torture and they won't have power over me anymore. I will do it as soon as I am out of here, and I will end it all."

Her voice rose to screaming again and then impulsively she threw the heavy leather bandage at the wall with all her strength. At almost the same moment, the door shot open and the alarmed orderlies appeared, ready to act.

"Everything is all right," I said to them as calmly as possible, but this time their trust in my professional authority was overpowered by the alarm they felt about this unbalanced patient. They closed the door only after I repeated myself. But their entrance had calmed Katherine down. She just breathed heavily and bit her lower lip, sitting tightly on her stretcher.

"Tell me, please, Katherine, the voices that you are hearing—what are they telling you?"

She stared at me, astonished.

"How do you know? I didn't tell anyone. I would never tell it to anybody. You can't possibly know that I hear them."

"I just guessed." There was no need to explain to her that her language itself revealed it. For a moment, she was immobilized by the necessity to make another choice. I saw clearly that she was balancing between breaking down in tears, telling her story in one breath, and falling down in uncontrolled outrage to avoid her feelings. This time she could turn violent. I had to intervene before her state of confusion moved in a dangerous direction.

"It's okay to talk about them. You have never tried to kill yourself before, either. So it's okay now to talk about your voices, especially because I know about them already."

"It's a girl. It's a little, little girl." She began talking. "She cries all the time, so endlessly and so desperately. I hear her crying constantly, somewhere in the back of my head. I can never see her, but I feel her and I feel how every time I make a move to hug her, to protect her, she pushes me away. And then she screams at me with hatred. 'It's all your fault! It's all your fault!' she screams at me and I can't stop her."

While Katherine was talking, she was also gasping for breath, and tears moved slowly down her cheeks. As she talked on, her speech went faster, her voice thinned, got higher, quicker, turned into a child's lament until her face was now that of a child, a lost, angry, and frightened girl who was clenching her fists, ready to hit anyone who would move closer.

"Katherine, I appreciate your talking to me, but before we go on I need to fill in some things in your papers. Can you tell me your address, please?"

I didn't have any intention of going any further on that dissociation trip.

She stopped abruptly, and then, in a different voice, told me her address, in the same mechanical way she would in any official situation. I knew that she was getting more and more tired, and I decided to finish this interview as soon as possible, especially because I already knew that she was dangerous to herself and that I had all the indications for holding her in the hospital. A few more questions, a prescription to ensure her good sleep, and I would be done. The therapy would be the task for day doctors coming in the morning.

"So because this voice tells you that you are guilty about something, you want to kill yourself?" She nodded her head.

"And you say that if I let you go now, you would go on with your plan?" Her silent nod was officially enough for me to end an interview and write down my consultation.

There was no need for me to go into the content of her traumatic experiences that were causing her depression and hallucinations. Her picture was clear. The management indicated was unambiguous. I had only to inform her of my decision and to go back to a few more hours of deserved rest before the morning round. But despite the obvious advantage of a few more hours of sleep, I didn't feel like rushing to it, quite surprisingly for myself, and I continued talking to Katherine, as if I was waiting for something else to emerge.

At that moment, I explained it to myself that to get up and leave her like that would be somewhat insincere on my part, as if I had deceitfully provoked her to tell me something intimate with the sole purpose of justifying my actions in admitting her involuntarily. At that moment, the explanation worked and I took it in without questioning, as a real one.

"And why do you believe that you are really guilty of something?" I asked, making an unsure step.

"Because she is right. It was my fault. It was all my fault. And I am the only one who is guilty of that."

"When you say 'that,' what exactly do you mean?"

Katherine looked at me again, as if checking the sincerity of my inquiry. She stayed silent for a while and then started talking, this time very slowly, carefully choosing her words, listening to those words herself as she pronounced them aloud for the first time.

"You know, doctor, I am very ashamed to talk about it. I don't even know how to say this. I have never tried to say it before. This is so shameful and so ugly." She was rocking her body back and forth rhythmically, as if trying to prompt herself by this movement to go on with her story. I didn't interrupt her anymore. I knew already what this story was going to be about, and I waited for her to finally let it out.

"I was raped. I was five years old when it happened. He was my uncle, from my mother's side. He was fifteen at that time, and I was only five. He took me to the cave outside my mother's house, and he did it there to me. I was so badly hurt, I couldn't walk for a few days. You know, I am still feeling a horrible pain from hip dislocation. I often have to take pain relievers. I was only five years old, but I remember every single detail, as if it happened yesterday. And when sometimes it seems to me that I have started to forget, it comes back in a dream. I see it again in my dreams, and then I am afraid to sleep for weeks. I have those flashes of fear that torture me when I go to bed. Sometimes I am afraid to close my eyes, afraid to see the details of that day, afraid to see his face over me again. I was only five years old, doctor."

She cried quietly. All her previous intensity, born mostly from the fight to keep this story away from her feelings, was gone. She cried openly and thanked me when I handed her a tissue.

"It's been tormenting me my entire life. I am thirty-nine years old now, and I haven't had a single happy day since that time. Look at me, doctor. I have nothing to live for, only the continuation of this torture. What for? About a year ago, I started to hear her cry. And then she started screaming that I am guilty. This girl, doctor, it's me, myself as that little five-year-old who was raped not far from her mother's house. I got so scared when I realized that this was my own voice shouting inside of me and that I didn't have any power to control it. Do you know, doctor, how frightening the thought is that you may be losing your mind? That thought was even scarier than the rape itself. That's why I never told anyone. It would be easier to kill myself than admit that I am going crazy."

She continued to sob, using one tissue after another to wipe her tears.

I felt she was telling the truth. But I had seen similar stories too often with sobbing, with suicide, with first-forgotten-but-then-suddenly-remembered child abuse, skillfully played by women craving attention, and sometimes simply craving drugs. So I had to be alert. I put aside her chart, got up from the chair, and came closer to her. I put my hand over Katherine's and said, "It's okay. It's really okay. It will be changed. You have started changing it already. You just need to be a little more patient and to work it out."

She was sobbing again like a little girl. I looked into her eyes and all my doubts were gone, but my calm was gone with them as well. There, behind the reddish space filled with tears, behind the dark brown center, behind the wide, black opening of the pupil, at the very bottom of her eyes, a lost little five-year-old girl was kneeling bare-legged on the ground, smashed by the pain and confusion of what her body had just gone through. And there was no one around to save her from that hurt; there was only the intimidating male figure leaning over her.

I pulled back, took her chart into my hands, pretending to read it, and thinking how often and to what extreme my profession had been stretching the limits of my endurance. I was thinking the same thought last morning, admitting a patient to my ward. He was a schizophrenic well known in the hospital, a former artist, gentle, intelligent man gradually succumbing to the destructive power of his disease. This time he came with new symptoms. He was detained by the police on the railroad track where he was walking toward a moving train. I knew him well. I even had a painting of his hanging on my office wall, a painting which he had done with exquisite technique many years ago during his first visit to the hospital.

"You know, doctor, my case today is me against the world. That's how I feel and that's how I will proceed from now on," he had said.

"Mr. Lavrov, it seemed to me in the past that we were able to understand each other well. Let me try to understand you this time. Can you help me please and explain what exactly you were doing walking toward the train?"

"You see, there is a riddle which I am bound to resolve. For the last five years, I can't comprehend exactly what kind of experience I am having. I think I am still alive, but there is an equal chance that I have been dead for all this time and that I am just stuck here between death and something else. And it is very possible that all my experiences now are some type of illusion imposed on me as a test. But what kind of test I don't know."

"So what were you trying to do in front of the train?"

"If the train went through me without changing anything, then I would know for sure I have been dead; if it killed me, I would know that I had been alive. It was supposed to bring clarity to my mind."

To give myself time to think if this unusual presentation could be considered a rare case of nihilistic Cotard's syndrome, and how much it was secondary to depression, I just told him:

"But you are alive, Mr. Lavrov. Believe me, you are alive. It is obviously so."

"What is so obvious about it?"

His answer actually interrupted my diagnostic effort and made me turn to him with more attention. I didn't know what to say.

He looked at the wall where his painting was displayed and contemplated it for a while. It was a masterful piece of work. Under the high, intensely blue sky lay a peaceful bed of green hills softly rolling away into the distance. The whole scene had a somewhat surreal, unearthly quality to it. The only reminders of human life in the picture were the rows of perfectly, almost photographically, depicted pairs of shoes, standing on the tops of the hills. There was every possible variety of shoes in all sizes, colors, styles. I am sure Mr. Lavrov conducted an extensive research into the history of shoes before doing his painting. The piece was called *Repressed Feelings*, and I liked it a lot.

"You see, doctor. It is probably obvious to you that my painting has a very deep symbolic significance. I am sure you have discussed with somebody how interesting it was for me to represent repressed feelings by absent bodies."

He was right. I had had such discussion with my colleagues at least twice.

"And it is pretty obvious to you. But it's not at all what I meant when I did it. I painted gravity. I painted the pull which our bodies constantly experience and which actually limits our feelings. I was thinking about experiences of weightlessness repressed by our density.

"So, coming back to our discussion, what is so obvious about me being alive and about everything and everybody around me being a reality but not an illusion? How can you prove that to me?" He turned to me with expectancy and rubbed his temples.

For a moment, my perception was torn apart by his sincere and uncompromising question. Somehow his question ripped my solid and grounded perception apart from the things themselves, and for that second, void of any material support, my perception was left thinned, enigmatic, weightless, and frighteningly vulnerable.

"The depression is first"; the saving thought came to me and glued my perception back to normal things. "Nihilistic ideas are secondary. So I will start with an antidepressant and a neuroleptic and will see how he is doing in a few days," I thought to myself.

But after Mr. Lavrov left my office, I couldn't stop thinking about the challenges of stretching myself in clinical encounters like that. His challenge was more intellectual, since it was his thinking that was distorted.

Meanwhile, Katherine's little girl was hitting my emotions, challenging the endurance of my professional detachment. I turned to her and continued:

"But why do you think that you are guilty for what happened?"

She hesitated and then started talking nonstop again, as if all in one breath, "I am guilty and it's my fault because I let him do it. He was the only one in the neighborhood who had a bike. I envied him so much. I never rode a bike. And my family never had enough money to afford one. I asked him to let me ride it, at least once. He was my uncle, after all. He said that he would give me the bike only if I did that thing with him. I didn't have any idea what thing he was talking about. I agreed and went with him to the cave. He put his jacket on the ground, pulled off my underwear and did it to me. I hurt so much, but more than the pain there was shame. I knew that I had done something horrible. I didn't say anything. He put me on the bike and rode me back to my house. I still remember pain from that bike. I have never ridden a bike since, and I have never told anybody."

She paused for a moment, and I felt that there was something else she needed to say.

"No, I spoke about it once. To my husband. We had been married for six months. And I had just started to feel safe and to not sense pain while we were having sex. I told him my story. I don't know what I expected from him when I did it. But what he did was worse than anything I could have imagined. He pulled me into the bedroom by my hair, and then he raped me. And while he was doing it he just kept saying, 'Is it how you felt then? Is it at all close to your first time?' I was in the hospital for two weeks with a pain syndrome after that. And I have never seen him since that day. We got divorced. My pain returned and has never left me since then. What do I have to live for in my life, doctor?"

"Katherine, you have to stay in the hospital. I can't let you go home now. And I hope very much that the doctor who comes in the morning will find the best way of helping you."

She looked even more scared.

"I don't want to stay here. I want to end it. You can't keep me here against my will."

"Yes, I can, Katherine. And I will. And someday you will thank me for it."

I left the examination room, went to the ER doctor's room, wrote down my consultation, and gave it to the doctor on-call.

"Admit her when she is medically stable. She is ours."

I didn't have to run back to my ward. The power of the cold to affect me was lost to all the emotions that were overwhelming me. Katherine was in such desperate need of help. I felt it in my very essence. She was begging for help with her unsophisticated means and I strove to help her. She was one of many faces with a similar story. I've heard this story before. I saw similar faces distorted by hurt before and I strove to help Katherine as much as I strove to help many other women before her. But the wall of helplessness stood in my way as it had in the past. I felt powerless in front of the depth from which her desperation arose. It was a well without bottom, a suffering which was always there for her. She didn't know any better. Where could I find the strength and knowledge to free her from that depth? I didn't have an answer.

But there was something else about my condition, something beyond my sympathizing with Katherine, that bothered me.

I walked slowly along the snow-covered path and registered how inside me a feeling of dissatisfaction and anxiety was growing. Used to introspection, I knew that there was something hidden behind my anxiety, something I was about to grasp, but I also felt that it was too big and too dangerous and it was eluding my awareness. So my mind passively agreed to let it go and not to try to find out why I felt anxious and uneasy. Somehow I felt that it was safer to let it go. So, for the time being, I did.

I walked on this snow-covered path in Siberia, and I didn't know then that far away in Uzbekistan, in the heart of Asia, under the walls of Samarkand, a few people came together and made a decision to act. I couldn't possibly know then, walking through the hospital grounds that night, that quite soon and unexpectedly, and without even knowing it, I would become a participant in the realization of that decision and that my anxiety and fears would serve as an engine taking me into spaces I didn't know existed.

Chapter 2

As usual, after broken, interrupted, on-call sleep which brought more exhaustion than rest, my day hours felt too long and almost never-ending.

But eventually even those long hours were over and I took my coat out of a closet, put it on, preparing to leave, going one more time in my mind through the orders I had made for my patients today, to make sure that everything was done and that I hadn't forgotten anything important before leaving.

I took my bag, ready to step out, when the door shot open and a girl walked in, confident and smiling, almost pushing me back in, as if she didn't have any doubts that I would be happy to see her. I didn't remember who she was. She looked so familiar and greeted me as her old friend, so that I felt quite stupid for not being able to remember where I had seen her before.

"Hi! I am Masha," she said in a low, melodic voice, and almost broke into laughter, enjoying my confusion.

"I am Masha," she repeated, emphasizing her name as if it was supposed to mean something special for me.

"You remember me? Don't you? You are Olga, right? We haven't met formally yet."

The fact that she wasn't sure who I was and something about her last phrase flashed through my memory and suddenly, her rosy face, her complexion, her tight-fitting jeans, the strength of her presence—it all came back to me in one picture and I remembered who she was. It was so unexpected and surprisingly pleasant to see her in my office that I threw my bag on the floor, took a seat in my favorite chair without taking off the coat, and sincerely said to her, "I am really glad to meet you formally, Masha. Thank you for coming. What can I do for you?"

She took a seat in front of me, took a cigarette out of her purse, and looked around for an ashtray. She did it so naturally and easily that I didn't say a word and just watched her, remembering the details of how I saw her the first time.

One night the phone rang in my apartment. It was late at night, so I expected it to be an emergency call. A deep, hoarse, man's voice said without introduction or apology for the late call and in an abrupt tone, "I want to speak to Olga. Are you she?"

"Yes. Who is calling?" I was trying to recognize this harsh voice belonging to someone phoning me at such a late hour, but it was definitely unfamiliar.

He continued in the same rude, patronizing tone, as if he hadn't even heard me.

"I have been told that you are quite an interesting girl, doing quite interesting things. Are you?"

"It depends on what things you would consider interesting. My guess is that we would have a different taste in that."

"Oh, I am sorry. I didn't apologize for calling so late and didn't even introduce myself. My name is Mr.

Smirnov. Your phone number was given to me by your colleague." He named a doctor working with me in the hospital. I cussed silently at a doctor who would give away home phone numbers without permission.

"How can I help you, Mr. Smirnov? If I can at all." His sudden transformation into a polite gentleman didn't trick me. His rude, harsh voice still sounded in my ears, causing waves of irritation in my body.

"We do psychological research in the city. I thought you may be interested to visit us. We live in the same city as you, and my belief is that all people of power should know each other and be connected."

His apparent flattery didn't ease my irritation with him, but increased it.

This is a guy who thinks his intelligence gives him a chance to manipulate everything. "Wrong assumption, Mr. Smirnov," an unpronounced dialogue continued in my head.

He kept talking. He told me about his laboratory and the research his people were doing there. I listened half-attentively, my mind occupied by its intense attempts to come to an understanding of this strange person. There was something else about this man, something that didn't allow me to just classify him as another power-seeking, smart manipulator, the well-known type inhabiting government-sponsored labs where they tried to penetrate the depth of human psyche with the sole purpose of pleasing their ambitious, bureaucratic bosses.

I couldn't avoid sensing the air of independence about him. His hoarse, deep voice was marked by a presence of profound awareness. My feeling that he possessed an exceptional power was mixed with a sense of real danger. It was a rare, attractive combination.

"Well, Mr. Smirnov, you have persuaded me that you are quite an interesting man, doing quite interesting things."

He laughed uninhibitedly loudly.

"You see, we have something in common already. Here is my address. This is my home and the lab at the same time." He dictated to me the street address and the directions for getting to the place by bus. I wrote it down, irritated with myself now by the fact that, after all, I was doing something at this man's command.

"Thank you. But I don't think that I will have time to pay you a visit soon. So I can't promise it to you."

"Of course you can't. And you don't have to. We will just be happy to see you. Good night."

I forgot about that weird call for a while, but a few days later my mind replayed the details of that conversation and I noticed a sense of anticipation which that memory caused in me. I tried to push away the impulse to go there, as it didn't seem a rational perspective, but anticipation changed quickly into anxiety, and I felt that it wouldn't go away until I visited his place. I felt as if his words promised to show me things about myself which I needed to remember but which I had postponed doing for a long time. After weighing all the pros and cons, I told myself finally that Mr. Smirnov seemed to be quite an extraordinary person such that I should not avoid a chance to meet him in person. I went to visit his lab.

The place was a thirty-minute bus ride outside the city. Novosibirsk, one of the largest cities on the Trans-Siberian Railroad, "the Heart of Siberia" as some people called it, was in fact a huge metropolis with a population of more than 1.5 million, with most people trying to live closer to its center, away from the industrial suburbs. People spent only their summer vacations in a community of country houses outside the city. I had never heard of anyone living there in winter.

Intrigued, I took the bus and looked for the address he gave me. To my surprise, the place was very easy to find. The bus stopped at an empty, snow-covered bus stop, surrounded on all the sides by a vast forest. I was the only one who got off the bus at that station. After walking a few hundred meters from the bus stop into the tall pine forest, following exactly the directions Mr. Smirnov gave me, I saw a large house, which differed greatly from the empty, wooden summer cottages which were scattered around the area.

It was an old Siberian house, built before the Revolution of 1917, probably in the late nineteenth century. I knew of only a few such houses that were left in the center of the city, and these were archeological relics. The rest of them were destroyed, giving way to many-storied apartment buildings, a foundation of common living.

The relic houses were built in the Tsar's time by the Siberian aristocracy who had enough resources to build for themselves beautiful, solid, massive buildings decorated in most cases with intricate woodcarving created by local masters.

This house was in a forest, surrounded by all the sounds, smells, and impressions one can't find in the city. It was silent and peaceful, with birds occasionally calling one another, the snow still lying white and untouched in this isolated place. In the city, it had already melted everywhere.

I walked slowly toward the house. As I approached, I paused in front of it for a while, enjoying its massive beauty. Darkened from time, oak logs lay in orderly rows constituting the high walls of the house. Intricate carvings surrounded the windows. A fairy-tale smoke was rising from an old chimney and was slowly dissipating behind tall evergreen trees covered by snow.

I needed time to adjust to this place which was so different from the hectic life of the city. I took a deep breath and knocked on the massive dark door, but my knock was absorbed by the old wood and seemed to be too weak to be heard inside the large house.

"Come in, it's open." A hollow voice replied from inside.

I opened the door and stood at the doorstep, undecided. Two wooden stairways faced me, one leading up and the other one down to the basement.

"Come down here, Olga." I heard Mr. Smirnov's voice and took the downward stairs, wondering how he could have known that it was me.

What I expected to be a basement was the first floor, as the house was built on the hillside and the entrance opened directly onto the second floor.

I paused at the last step before making the final step down to the wooden floor which was covered with oriental rugs. A man standing on the opposite side of the room turned toward me. I couldn't see his face clearly. He stood near the window, lit by the bright outside light so that I was looking at him against the light. His silhouette was graphically depicted against the window glass as a tall, slightly stooped, black figure, intense in its motionlessness. Yet the next moment he moved quickly and walked through the room, extending his hand to me. "Nice to meet you finally."

He offered me his hand as a support to walk down from the last step instead of expecting me to shake it. I delayed for a moment and looked again with attention at this strange room. The room was a large living hall. The high oak bookshelves dominated the room, running from floor to ceiling, even made round at the corners, creating an illusion that the whole room was circular. An empty antique rocking chair covered with a dark brown cashmere throw was swinging slightly in front of the wood-burning stove, as if somebody had just sat in it a moment ago.

Three identical doors were closed but suggested the entrances to other rooms. There was no other furniture in the room, except for one small table placed against the window. It had a pile of papers on it and a plastic chair stood beside it.

The strange components of the room created confusion. Expensive, exquisite rugs on the floor; old, rare manuscripts; the complete writings of Russian classics; and piles of books in foreign languages displayed behind glass suggested the owner had unlimited resources. Yet the amount of dust in the room, the naked window without drapery, the relative absence of furniture, the traces of coal on the parquet floor around the stove, all showed a lack of care for this house and were to me somehow troubling.

I took Smirnov's hand and stepped down off the ladder. His face now was in front of me, and I could see him clearly. He looked strikingly familiar. I was almost sure we had met before. He had a pronounced Semitic nose, his dark brown eyes emitted an intense gaze, and with his thick eyebrows and wrinkles covering his face he looked familiar. The kindness of his manners and his deep slow voice enhanced this perception and created in me a basic trust in him, despite my initial doubt.

"Would you like a glass of wine?" he suggested cheerfully.

It wasn't a Russian custom to suggest a glass of wine in the middle of the day, except at lunch or dinner.

"No, thank you," I said as my sense of guardedness returned, summoned by his unexpected suggestion.

"You think I am tricky, don't you?"

"Are you not?"

"I guess I may be, but not now. I want to create a serious impression with you, and there is a reason why I want to do so."

"That's a very tricky expression in itself," I commented.

"Yes, that's probably right," he laughed slightly, and I noticed how quickly his laughing dissolved my uneasiness again.

"I'd like to invite you to my office before giving you a tour of my center."

He opened one of the three doors and we entered a small room that didn't have any windows, and was lit by an artificial light coming from the ceiling. There was a table covered with piles of paper with photocopied diagrams on them. Behind the table, on the wall, hung a huge oil portrait of a naked woman sitting on a chair. She was looking at me with full awareness in her gaze of what a shocking impression her image was causing.

"This is my wife," said Smirnov in a casual tone. "She is going to bring us some tea in a moment." The woman in the portrait was almost unnaturally beautiful. Her graceful body was classically proportioned, her thick, black hair fell freely on white shoulders, and her eyes were full of the awareness that she was exquisitely beautiful.

Above the portrait, there was a white ribbon fixed along the wall upon which a phrase was painted with red letters: "Everything is Communicating." The logo was as strange as the portrait.

"Here she is," said Smirnov when the door on the other side of the room opened and a woman walked in, carrying a silver tray with a teapot and two cups.

"Meet my wife, Anastasia," said Smirnov.

The woman carefully placed the tray on the table and extended her small hand to me for a handshake. I was shocked, and it took me a moment to react to her outstretched hand. The woman standing in front of me had nothing whatsoever to do with the glowing beauty still looking at us from the wall. In person, she was a typical Russian middle-aged housewife, of small height, plump, with gray unkempt hair and no makeup, glasses resting on her inexpressive face. I shook her hand and, while trying to be nice, I still couldn't avoid switching my gaze from her to the portrait. Anastasia caught my move, and because I clearly was not the first one confused by the discrepancy, she laughed readily and then said in a soft voice, "It's true. It's me. And it's true that everything is about communicating. Communicating is magic. This is a truly magical portrait."

She paused for a moment and then said before leaving the room, "I know how to change."

With these words she left the room, leaving me with her husband, who didn't try to hide the delight my confusion had caused in him.

I took a cup of tea from the silver tray, just to take a moment to ease the situation and to hold myself from a burning desire to find out what this performance meant.

"Let me tell you something," Smirnov said, leaning over the desk and looking at me with a serious and somewhat intimidating expression.

The sip of tea was too hot, so I took it carefully, waiting for him to continue.

"The real similarity between us is . . ." He paused and kept looking straight into my eyes, making me feel that the bottom of the discomfort I thought I had reached a moment ago wasn't really a bottom, but just a surface. I didn't have any intention to jump into it, so I took another sip of tea and remained silent.

"See? You don't want anybody to impose their rules on you. I suggest a dialogue to you and you stubbornly shut up. If I wasn't talkative, you probably would put into use all your psychiatric techniques to make me tell you more."

"Probably," I was ready to pronounce, but found to my surprise that to keep looking at him silently and to drink my tea felt to be a much more comfortable response.

He laughed again.

"It is about freedom, Olga. It is a thirst for freedom which makes us so similar. To try to play by your own rules is only the tip of the iceberg that carries you through life. The iceberg's real body consists of tons of buried intentions, decisions, feelings, ambitions, different in their character but still drifting as one body in one direction: the remote island that has a huge sign displayed at its edges. It says 'FREEDOM' in capital letters. You don't want to turn a millimeter away from that destination."

"You like slogans, don't you?" I said, feeling that I was much more ready to break the conversation apart than to hold it up, and I was asking myself what I was doing in this weird place and why on earth had I come here?

"Mind has different forms of expressions. Slogans are great forms of expression which can impress at the same time." And then, without transition, he asked, "Now, do you want me to show you around?"

I carefully placed my china cup back on the silver tray and silently followed Smirnov, who opened the door to the living room without giving me the chance to respond to his offer.

The structure of this house was unusual. It seemed that one large living room had entrances to various smaller rooms which didn't have any connection to one another. Two more doors besides the one to his office which led to the other rooms were still closed. Smirnov stood in the middle of the living room and looked at me, the joker in his eyes winking to me again.

"So which one of these doors do you want to open first?"

At this moment, I realized why this man's behavior was so irritating. Somehow he sensed correctly my striving for freedom and independence as underlying qualities of my character. He was using this to his own purposes when he didn't give me a choice, and manipulated this quality of mine to make me play by his rules.

"You are the master of this house, Mr. Smirnov. I am a guest, so I will follow you."

He smiled as if that was the only response he had expected from me and, after a minute of pretended indecisiveness, he made a step toward the door on his right, located opposite his office.

All this had caused anticipation in me and, I had to admit, while following him through the opening door, his techniques worked. I felt somehow impressed, so my expectations of what would happen next were much higher than if he had taken me on an ordinary tour around his laboratory.

When he opened the door and started into the next room, his movements changed and his gestures and the whole stature of his body assumed a different dynamic. He was now walking almost on the tips of his toes, trying to make as little noise as possible, and trying to be very careful in his movements and expressions.

I followed him and entered a somewhat darkened room in which, at first, I couldn't see anything. But as my eyes adjusted, I saw a large space, and that room was only slightly smaller than the living room.

It was hard to say if the room had any windows, since its walls were covered with rich black velvet. There were two large mirrors placed on opposite walls. Their surfaces reflected bluish light coming from small floor lamps.

Where the beams from the different lamps crossed, I saw two heavy wooden chairs placed in front of each other, as if two people were supposed to sit in them facing each other and have an important discussion. But instead of these two imaginary people, what I saw there was much more troubling. I saw a woman's body lying between these chairs. The back of her head was supported by a soft cushion on the left chair, and her feet were fixed where a second imaginary person would sit. Her body had only these two points of support—the back of her head and her feet—and looked to be floating in space, weightless and petrified.

Even though I have attended sessions of popular traveling hypnotists who performed more sophisticated tricks than this, the unpleasant sensation of this scene was powerful. The girl was beautiful and very young, probably not even in her twenties. Her face and figure were not particularly gentle. She had a bright, ruddy beauty such as one would expect from a healthy village girl who grew up nourished by nature and unspoiled by civilization. She had wide cheekbones, a sturdy nose, beautifully outlined lips, dark wide eyebrows which framed her closed eyes, and she had a shock of thick, long black hair framing her face.

She was dressed casually in a pink tee shirt and blue jeans that fit tightly over her well-built torso. She slept with a quiet, healthy sleep as if she were lying in her goosedown bed at home, comfortable and relaxed. She reminded me of the heroine of a Russian folktale who had been mesmerized and bewildered by an evil sorcerer and hidden away in his empty, cold castle to serve a cruel purpose of which only he was aware. As if to support my impression, Smirnov came closer to her, reminding me even more strongly of the fairytale's sorcerer. He leaned over her sleeping body and contemplated her features, trying to notice the slightest changes. He then pulled back, reassured when he saw that she was calm and wasn't even moving, and that her enchantment was unbroken even after our entrance.

I took a few steps closer and looked at her from this perspective. When I did so, Smirnov leaned to her again and lightly touched a little birthmark on her face in the middle of her left cheek. His touch was gentle, but somehow it looked like he touched more than skin, reaching his index finger into the deepest muscles of her face. At the same time, he touched it as if he kissed her with his finger. This was weird. He pushed harder on her face and she responded by taking a deep breath and then holding her breath for a while before returning to her slow rhythm of sleep breathing.

Reassured that everything looked as it was supposed to, Smirnov gestured, showing me that we could leave then through another door in front of us and opposite the entry door.

I didn't have a chance to look closer at her, but despite her uninterrupted unresponsiveness and her deep sleep, there was a strong sensation that she somehow became aware of our entrance and especially of my presence, knowing there was somebody present who was new, who was a stranger and different from Smirnov, the master her body knew.

Before walking out, I saw a dark brown piano in the corner of the room behind the two chairs and the sleeping girl. I wondered if the piano was there as a leisure-time entertainment or if it was used for hypnotic inductions for people who got to go through this room and lie on those chairs.

As we were leaving the room, Smirnov's gait changed again and returned to his previous relaxed, careless pattern. I couldn't help but notice that his walking through the room with the hypnotized girl, his attentiveness, and all the nuances of his behavior in that room, showed how important this girl and her condition were for him and how significant it was for him to preserve that condition. He almost forgot about me while looking at the girl and checking changes in her, noticeable and understandable only to him. While doing so, he exhibited complete concentration. Watching him walk through that room and have that short communication with the girl, I understood that this was something he cared about, something in which he invested a lot of energy, something on which he was almost dependent. I couldn't help but wonder why it was so important for him, but I couldn't find an answer.

We entered another room that finally fit the initial description Smirnov had used for this place. It was a real "lab" with three light plastic tables placed in a row near the wall. Large computer monitors stood on each table, their illuminated screens flashing rhythmically. There was no one in the room. But the subtle sounds of working computers and their blue screens created an impression that the computers lived their own lives, knew their jobs well, and performed them without any human interference.

Many electrical cords attached to the computers connected them together and to the metal clips lying on the tables. Altogether it reminded me of an EEG lab, but more advanced than the ones I knew. In support of this impression, a narrow black couch stood near the wall, implying that at least once in a while the work performed in this room involved people lying on the couch.

"This is my pride," commented Smirnov, gesturing toward the row of computers. "The achievement of a lifetime, if you wish. You may be interested to learn more about this program. People of your profession and . . ." he made a pause and then continued, ". . . of your personality type can find this work very interesting." He came closer to one of the monitors that had an oblong shape depicted on its blue surface.

"Here we map the brain, hoping to map the mind," he continued. "We record electrical signals of brain activity and then the program analyzes them and shows the brain's infrastructure at work. We are looking to understand the focus of awareness. The seat of attention, if I may say. We believe that when we understand that, our possibilities will become unlimited."

I looked at the screen. Inside the perfect oval a few little stars pulsated, rhythmically turning from points to stars and then back to little points.

"You are seeing the points of awareness recorded before. The program analyzed and saved it. It is the brain activity of the girl from the other room. Her name is Masha. She worked here some time ago while experiencing a particular state. Isn't it fascinating to see how technology can particularize our experiences, preserving Masha's condition here while she is absorbed in a totally different experience now? I find it as challenging as transcending time itself. And this is only the beginning of what we plan to do. But look here, at this monitor, Olga. Don't you notice anything strange?"

I looked at the screen. It looked unfamiliar but I couldn't see anything strange.

"Not really," I replied.

"Are you sure? Look more carefully."

"Why don't you just tell me what you mean, Mr. Smirnov? It will save us time so we wouldn't have to transcend it."

He laughed softly and looked at me very kindly, almost as if I was his close relative lost long ago and finally found.

"Because it would take the fun out of it. Try to get it yourself," he said in a soft voice.

It wasn't a very noticeable change in the tone of his voice, but it made an impact on me. I felt a warm wave of anticipation inside caused by the subtle softness of his voice as if it promised to tell me something secret and significant.

"We are dealing here, Olga, with the deepest mystery of our existence, with our miraculous subjectivity, with our ever-elusive self which is always there and which has never been really understood. We put much effort into describing persona and its different dynamics. But persona is not self even though we are conditioned to think so. They are qualitatively different phenomena." He paused for a while and then continued in a slower rhythm. "Persona is a cloud and rather a small one despite our efforts to inflate it. And this cloud flies above the vast land called the mind of *Homo sapiens*. This land has flower fields and dark forests, deserts, and mountains, and a little lake. This is the land I want to map with this program." His gaze was fixed on the computer screen as he continued talking.

"You learn how to scatter the cloud of persona and see what is left. This is what we record here. The point of real self, the seat of awareness. Now do you see anything strange here?"

His speech made me feel much closer to the pulsating blue screen. It reflected his words on its lit surface somehow, and the space on the screen encompassing the twinkling stars felt as if it was preserving inside of it Masha's experience afresh even though she wasn't here.

The feeling of mystery touched me and generated an immediate insight. I knew in a moment what he was asking about.

"There are several of them. There are several stars on the screen while she has one isolated experience. Is that what you mean? There is more than one self; there are multiple points of subjectivity."

"You got it," he agreed, obviously pleased with my response. Then he commented, "But not every experience generates this picture. None of our daily conditions would record like this. No matter how much inner babbling, confusion, or doubts one has, there is always only one dominant center that is the point of awareness for that particular moment. What Masha experienced here was a variation of sleep paralysis. It is a part of her natural experience which I helped her to develop. She can't move her muscles; she can't talk at those times. Vivid images come up into her consciousness and she experiences them as realistically as if they were in this very room communicating with her. Then the program records the presence of multiple selves. Much to think about." He looked excited talking about it.

I thought about Masha submitting herself to these experiments and couldn't avoid questioning, "How does she feel at those times? Does she like it, or does it feel scary to her?"

Smirnov's face relaxed after he heard my question, making him more distant and detached again. "It feels more scary than not. But there is not much choice. We have to do it." He gave me this evasive answer and gestured toward the door, letting me know that our time in this room was up.

I followed him out, knowing that I couldn't expect any more details from him.

After that room we came straight to a large kitchen, with a wide, massive oak table in the middle and a huge stove with a few pots on it. Anastasia stood near one large pot in which boiling food emitted a wonderful aroma, making this house and its strange inhabitants seem cozy, familiar, and trustworthy.

At the corner of the table sat two young men, sipping red wine from large glasses and eating sausages. A pile of burned cigarettes filled the cast-iron ashtray between them. They examined us briefly as we walked in, and it was obvious that the presence of somebody new was routine in this place. Nobody paid any further attention to me.

Smirnov gestured to me to sit at the other side of the table, away from the talking men. He nodded his head in their direction and told me softly before taking his seat, "The man on my left is Victor, one of our best operators. And on the right from you is our American friend visiting from California. His name is Phil." Both guys looked very much alike, except Phil reminded me of a young Brad Pitt who had suddenly lost all of his glamour being transported from sunny California to Siberia and felt confused because of it. Victor looked like his Russian counterpart who never had any glamour and didn't care.

Victor looked at me briskly and made an indefinite move of his head, as if greeting me quickly. Phil smiled at me politely, but was prompted by Victor's brisk speech to return to his previous dialogue with Victor.

Phil tried to carry on in Russian, and he tried to speak fast, to keep up with Victor's brisk rhythm to show he was fluent in Russian. But because he was not, he had to stop quite often and correct himself or find different words.

"So, Olga . . . What do you think so far?" Smirnov asked me, lowering his head so that his brown eyes were right at the level of mine. He looked at me without blinking, his facial expression not showing any sign of what he was thinking.

"What do I think of what?"

"Of our place, our work, our people? Do you think anything about it?" He sounded as if he was trying to be casual.

"I don't think I've seen enough to come to any kind of conclusion. It's definitely an unusual place, and the people you have here seem like interesting people. But I don't have any idea what you do here."

I noticed that Victor, who sat across the table on the left side from Smirnov, looked at me quickly. I knew he had registered my answer somehow. The look lasted only a moment and then he returned to his animated conversation with Phil.

"We do different things," Smirnov continued in a lower voice. "We help people to get better."

"That sounds promising. This is the kind of job that I try to do. So tell me how you do yours."

He paused for a while, still looking at me directly, and even though I sensed that his gaze was supposed to make me feel uncomfortable, surprisingly, I felt calm. "I guess I have adjusted to his style already," I thought to myself.

"You saw Masha in the other room?"

"It would be hard not to notice her."

"She is an extraordinarily gifted young woman who would be completely lost if it wasn't for us. She would probably be drunk right now at the train station, humiliated by jerks, probably sick, and thinking how to do away with herself, if it wasn't for us—for the support and care she receives here."

"So, lying on the chairs is a therapeutic session, right?" I asked Smirnov, even though it would be very difficult for me to believe it.

"No, it isn't." Smirnov said, confirming my thinking. "She is working for me. She is doing a particular type of work that can give some therapeutic effect for her as well, but her goal right now is different. What I am saying is that even by merely being with us, by being a part of our group, sharing our goals and our vision, she is getting healed. And she was in need of a lot of healing, believe me, from all those scars, which, even though invisible, cover her throughout her body and soul."

I noticed how Victor made another quick look at us while still talking to his partner. At the moment I met his gaze, I could hear him saying across the table, "You are absolutely right. This is our goal and this is our mission. And we believe that we may find very interested partners on the other side of the ocean who share the same goals and beliefs and who would be very interested to see our results."

I couldn't hear what Phil answered since Smirnov resumed talking to me.

"This is the whole idea, making people comfortable and healed so that they can start becoming helpful to larger groups of people. We work mostly with human perception, trying to decipher the geometrical patterns that organize perception, and we learn how to change those patterns into better ones. We use different tools for that, both physical and psychic. In Masha's case, I am repairing the hurt left in her by her family. She told me things she would never tell anyone. She let me know about the stuff she went through that she wasn't fully aware of herself until she spilled it out one day when we talked. And now here she is—a gifted, helpful person, content and self-confident with energy other people can only dream about. Isn't it a nice transformation?"

"I hope it is."

"Do you have any doubts about that?"

"No, I don't have any doubts about that." I heard an enthusiastic answer coming now from Phil, as if he had heard Smirnov's question. But when I looked at him I could see that he just continued his separate conversation with Victor.

"I don't have any doubts." Phil repeated. "I know . . . I know you are right . . . right there. I am just asking why you don't show more? Why don't you show me more so I can understand you better?" His voice sounded unsure and his Russian got noticeably worse as he spoke.

"Why don't you tell me more?" I asked Smirnov.

"I can tell you whatever you want to know. Do you know what you really want to know?"

"Well, what is the purpose of this place? Is this a healing center? Is it a research center? Are you a social-service organization?"

"We are all those things together. We do all of those things with efficiency."

After a short pause he continued, "Why don't you pay us a few more visits and maybe participate in some of our activities so you can see for yourself how helpful we can be and how helpful you can be working with us."

"Thank you. But frankly, I don't feel comfortable with this idea. I probably can come up with some explanation for my answer. And I understand it is probably not nice to tell a person who invites you to be a guest that you are not comfortable being a guest, but this is exactly how I feel. I want to be honest with you, Mr. Smirnov. I do appreciate your inviting me, and showing me a little of what is going on here, but I can't see any possibility that I could be involved in your projects and work."

"Some people are afraid to be healed. You know that, right?"

"Right. It's not the case with me. I just don't feel comfortable with this. That's all. That's all it is. Besides, I don't have much to be healed from."

"Is that right?"

"You will feel much more comfortable with everything that goes on here," said Victor, who kept talking. As striking as this phrase sounded, as if he was answering me, when I looked at him, I saw that he was still talking to Phil.

"It is not a matter of being comfortable or uncomfortable," Phil interrupted briskly. "It is a matter of me trying to understand the way you live, the way you work, the way you experience yourself, and the other stuff around you. You know, I am not particularly good at finances or networking. The business thing is exactly what I ran away from, exactly what I was trying to escape. Yet here I am, in Siberia, for God's sake, gullible and open, and you are trying to feed me the same shit I didn't enjoy in California." Phil's Russian deteriorated with every phrase so that the final few sentences spilled out in his native English.

"All right. Take it easy. Take it easy." Now it was Smirnov who spoke to Phil in perfect English.

"Experience is prime here. You know that. You found good friends here in Siberia, and you'll get the exact experience you came to look for. We are not pushing anything here. It is not our style."

Suddenly, I didn't feel like continuing the conversation. I knew that I could have asked Smirnov a lot of practical questions, but I felt suddenly so tired—without any obvious reason—that I didn't feel like staying there any longer. I felt I wanted to leave the house as soon as possible. Smirnov, probably sensing my intention somehow, started to talk to his wife, who was still busy cooking. They talked in soft voices, but I felt that the words they exchanged were addressed to me and Phil. They discussed the details of "an important guest" coming in today. The guest was flying in from somewhere in Central Asia, and Smirnov sounded very excited about finally being able to meet him. Apparently, Smirnov had spent a lot of time trying to contact this person in Uzbekistan, and had finally given up hope of finding him. It was then that the person himself contacted Smirnov and suggested a visit to Novosibirsk. Smirnov and Anastasia clearly expected his visit to be an extraordinary experience.

"Even though I haven't seen him before, I have heard great things about him and his group. The guy is supposed to be brilliant and his work is pure healing. I am sure you would enjoy meeting him." Smirnov addressed his last phrase directly to me.

But somehow I didn't like the idea of staying there longer. I didn't like the idea of having come there in the first place. I felt that my expectations were not fulfilled. I didn't learn or remember anything insightful about myself on account of being there. My recent anxiety, the source of which I was trying to find by coming here, intensified instead of dissolved, and after the few hours I spent in his house, Smirnov seemed devoid of mystery. I decided to leave. They didn't insist on my staying longer.

I said good-bye and left the kitchen. Victor, finishing his conversation with Phil, walked me to the front door at Smirnov's request. Without Smirnov's presence, he was much more relaxed, less pompous, and seemed younger than I first had guessed. He was like a tall, grown-up boy who still played his imaginary childish games after everybody had granted him adult status.

He didn't say anything to me until we reached the door. But before I opened it to leave, Victor held my sleeve and gazed into my eyes with teenage directness and said quickly with no interruptions, "Do you know, Olga, or have you ever felt, that when you look straight at the sun for some time—look straight at the center until everything in your mind goes red and the sun disk turns black—that if you close your eyes, the disk starts pulsating and approaches you? That if you stay very still, very, very still, you hear the noise, like a gate opening, and you enter it, and you can ride horses on the surface of the sun itself and travel through it wherever you want to?"

"Is he giving drugs to these kids or something?" I thought to myself, leaving the house, not answering Victor's strange question.

This thought made me remember Masha, her rigid and defenseless body, lying between the chairs. I felt I almost knew her, even though I was sure I hadn't seen her before. I had a strange feeling as if it was dangerous to leave her there in that closed velvet room and as if I was responsible for having left her there in danger without doing anything for her.

I felt strangely guilty making my way back through the snow to the bus stop. I walked slowly through the snowy path toward the bus station. Suddenly, a new, white Toyota van turned sharply off the main highway and sped toward me on its way to the house, as easily as if it were a clean road and not a snow-packed, tough Siberian track.

It drove fast, and I had to jump off the road to let the car through. I had time only to notice that there were many people in the car, five at least. I didn't see their faces, but one man was sitting by the window and was looking straight at me as the car flashed by. His face I saw in detail. It was a face of an Asian man with dark skin, further darkened by a full beard, with large almond-shaped eyes; his head was covered by a high, white silk turban. I saw his face behind the car window only a few moments, but he looked at me directly. He *saw* me, and I felt such a presence behind his eyes that his image got into me and stayed with me for a long time on my way back, as if he were riding with me in the empty bus that took me back to the city. It was the man Smirnov expected to arrive from the airport, I was sure. At that moment, I couldn't appreciate the significance of his arrival. I was just impressed by his exotic look and I soon forgot about him until later.

Chapter 3

Masha, the hypnotized girl from Smirnov's strange house, was sitting in front of me, looking for an ashtray and behaving as if my office was one of her many homes or at least soon would be. I felt glad to see her. As I watched her, the feeling of recognition emerged strongly again, bringing up with it the anxiety from something I had been trying to remember but couldn't.

"Hi again," she said, smiling with the most charming smile one could imagine. I bet she had exercised that smile for many years now, so confident she looked in her childish spontaneity.

"I guess I was right in time to catch you." She nodded her head toward my bag, which I had tossed on the floor.

The moment Masha spotted an ashtray on another table, she suddenly changed her mind. She lost interest in smoking without any obvious reason, and put her cigarette back in the chest pocket of her brown leather jacket.

The heaviness of her features was counterbalanced by her eyes, which were dark-brown, sly, and suggestive of much more experience than I would have expected from one her age. She was very comfortable to be around. She immediately created an impression of being an open, communicative, sweet girl who was straightforward and defenseless—who was a lot of fun to spend time with, and yet who also needed to be cared for and protected because she was too vulnerable in her openness. The presence of much insight in her eyes showed me that the persona she was so used to playing wasn't all she truly was. But what else was she besides this lovely disguise?

I didn't even want to guess, for I felt intuitively that she barricaded that territory of herself not only with the smiling face of a charming girl but with techniques she had created and would use mercilessly against anyone who would try to get to those parts of her that were prohibited. I sensed this was Smirnov's territory, that from this space he ruled her, and because of this intuition I had even less intention to explore her hidden side. That she was a fun-loving, energetic woman-child was good enough for me at this time.

"I came to invite you to our lab," Masha said, looking at me with a naïve expression in her brown eyes. "I told them you wouldn't decline the invitation," she added after a slight pause. The few phrases she pronounced were enough to prompt me to start talking to her as to a child. She did this somehow with her voice, with her intonation, with her overly relaxed pose. Her eyebrows were arched as if in question and her face seemed liable at any moment to lapse into worry. Nobody, of course, would want to hurt the feelings of such a nice, good-hearted, but insecure girl.

"Masha . . . please . . ." I said to her as if I had known her for a long time. She understood me right away and changed her expression as if her face was made of a very elastic substance and my words were a force which could reshape it at once. I didn't have any intention to go back to that house.

"Okay. Seriously. We sent invitations to some people. But it is going to be a closed event. Smirnov sent me to tell you about it, because you said that you were interested in healing, which I guess you are," she said and looked around my office.

"Vladimir is giving a lecture tonight, his last one before leaving with a group to Samarkand. When Smirnov said that this guy was brilliant, I thought at first it was his new trick. I couldn't believe that he was serious because never before had I heard him say 'brilliant' about anybody. But he seemed serious about working with Vladimir after all, and he really is brilliant. The healing he did in our lab was very impressive. He could do things I had never seen before. And believe me, I have seen a lot." I believed her.

"Did Vladimir do any work with those computers I saw in your lab?" I asked Masha, feeling that I could talk to her straightforwardly.

"The computers? You saw them, eh? I call those pictures on the screen 'self-portraits.' Did you do any work with them?" She asked this question with a hint of jealousy, as if she was concerned that somebody else could have taken her place even if only for a short time.

"No, I didn't," I answered calmly and waited for her to continue.

"I think Vladimir saw it. I bet you heard a lecture from Smirnov in that room about the little cloud of our persona?" She sounded ironic now.

I just nodded silently.

"Did you believe it?"

"Believe what? He used a metaphor. A metaphor is not something you would believe or not. It was just a symbol." I couldn't see her point.

"Did you believe that was his intention—to scatter away the cloud of persona and to reach an understanding of the real self? Good for you if you did. I have heard his metaphor many times. When I heard it for the third time I told myself, 'He wouldn't repeat it so often if he really believed it.' And then I looked at him carefully and I got it. The only thing Smirnov is looking for in that room is exactly the opposite. He can let go of persona easily—mine or somebody else's. But not his.

"What he is searching for is how to preserve that cloud of his persona for as long as possible. He is terrified by the inevitability of death. He pretends to be patient, but in reality he is desperate. He is searching for immortality and he will do anything to get the key to it to save his persona. That's why Vladimir's visit is so important for Smirnov. From what he has heard about Vladimir from people who have met him before, Smirnov believes that Vladimir has the key to immortality, or at least knows where it is hidden. Because of that, he takes Vladimir very seriously. So are you coming for the lecture?" she returned abruptly to her original question.

I looked at her with a smile, not knowing what to answer.

"You have to come, Olga. I told them you wouldn't decline the invitation. Smirnov was insistent on your coming. He doesn't send me too often to invite people in, as you can guess. And besides, I came by car and I can take you, and then, after the lecture, bring you home so you won't have to stand in an overfilled bus."

That proposition I couldn't decline. I felt in a moment how tired I was after the busy night in the hospital. Going by car instead of bus sounded so good that going back to Smirnov's lab seemed like something very easy to tolerate.

So we drove back to the city in her red Jeep, a type of a car which only the richest people in the city could afford at that time.

Masha was a wild driver, passing all the cars on the snowy road in such a rude manner that it looked as if she was taking a personal revenge against every driver.

Still, we arrived late. When we entered the familiar house, the hall room was already full with people and the lecture had started. People were sitting on chairs in the middle, on the floor near the walls, and some were cozily perched on the window sills. Even though the room was full, it repeated its initial impression on me as being large but empty.

Vladimir stood opposite the entrance door, at the same place where Smirnov had stood the first time I entered this house. Golden draperies, which had not been there at my first visit, were drawn over the large window, and the room was lit with a soft light. Vladimir interrupted his monologue when Masha and I entered the room, and he remained silent while we found seats.

He was the man I had seen behind the window of the white Toyota. He wore the same white silk turban as the first time I saw him. He was looking at me intently, yet his gaze didn't have any of the tension Smirnov's had at our first meeting. His eyes were intensely focused on me, but there was no intent to impress or influence me. He was just communicating in his own powerful way, and it felt very comfortable to me.

The moment Masha and I took our seats, Vladimir continued talking. He spoke in a low voice with an unusual accent created more by the rhythm of his talking than by his style of pronunciation.

I leaned toward Masha and asked her in a whisper, "What is the name of his presentation?"

"Healing the Spirits of Trauma."

Vladimir's pose was elegant. He almost didn't move, yet held his figure, dressed in a completely buttoned-up blue silk costume, with grace and energy.

"You know I have traveled a lot. The main thing that fascinates me everywhere I go is one particular thing that everybody has in common. Everybody on this planet wants to be happy. Another common thing I have seen is that it is quite difficult for most of the people to get there, to their happiness. People before me have wondered why that is so. I have a different answer than what many people have said. It is not my personal insight which I am going to share with you. I belong to a group of people practicing a tradition of healing, a very ancient tradition, as I told you before. My goal today is to introduce you to the main principles of our work. I understand most of the people in this room are involved, one way or the other, in the practice of healing.

"Can you tell me what, from your judgment and experience, you consider to be the source of suffering and unhappiness in the world?"

A wave of movement went through the audience. I looked around and saw mostly young people, while a few academic-type older men sat in a first row. People looked at one another, waiting to see who would answer, and then I heard Masha's low voice pronounce with a slight giggle, "Is it evil?"

Vladimir looked at her momentarily with the same unusual attention I noticed in his eyes before, then continued, "When you say 'evil,' it is a powerful statement. But this statement also distances you from the source. It's like you cut yourself off, or cut off everything which is good in yourself from the nature of evil, and you think that through that, you can achieve healing and protection.

"In reality, it is vice versa. When you distance yourself from the source of suffering, when you name it as opposite to what you want to be (I assume that you all want to be good, don't you?), you lose a chance to change it. Because it continues to live inside you, as part of you, making you make many of your choices, but you refuse to recognize it, so you remain in ignorant bliss and you continue to suffer.

"We call the source of unhappiness and disease 'trauma.' And we believe that there are live representations of trauma in all of us. In our tradition, we call them 'spirits of trauma.' Whenever something hurts you and you don't accept it fully as a complete part of your history, you create a gap in your memory; a gap which, when the hurt is strong or repeated many times, becomes occupied by a spirit of trauma. You don't have to imagine some old-fashioned freaky monster sitting on your back and sucking out your blood." A ripple of soft laughter went through the audience as an expression of relief.

"You can think about this in terms of neurocognitive science, if you like the term 'neurotransmitters' better than 'creatures of the night.' You may call them additional subjects; you may define them as unintegrated representations; you may choose whatever language and metaphors you prefer. It doesn't matter. What matters is the process. The internal psychic *process*, often extended throughout generations by the inheritance of patterns of trauma formed, perhaps long, long ago, when one of your ancestors went through an unbearable hurt.

"Human genes are much more flexible than we think. They perceive as much as they act. When a hurt reaches the level of genes, it makes them behave differently and distort the memory, preventing the memory from becoming complete. The gap in memory is created, and a spirit of trauma houses itself in this gap, hidden from our awareness.

"The spirit of trauma is at work when you have a man who has a great family, a nice life, mental stability, then one day, all of a sudden, he gets up in the morning, leaves a note to his wife, kisses his eleven-year-old son good-bye, goes to the cemetery with a razor in his pocket. And on the grave of his father, who hung himself when this man was exactly eleven years old, he cuts his throat. He cuts it so deep that when the police find him, the grave is soaked in his blood, and it takes a medical miracle to bring him back from death. And when he is brought back he can't explain what happened. He doesn't have any clue, except that he felt so sad for his father, he wanted to be with him.

"It is an extreme scenario. But you know what? People have much deeper tragedies in their family histories than you could ever imagine. They learn to hide them from themselves and their children. They play hide-and-seek with spirits of trauma, and guess what? Most often they lose, because even when they don't remember, their genes—those unfailing memory units—do, and the hurt stays there until you heal it.

"The same mechanism works with smaller things. We start to gather up more personal hurts in the basket of our memory soon after coming into this world. The way it continues is in accordance with Darwin's ideas about the survival of the fittest, but it's extended to psychic realities. Every creature tries to survive. It is true for the spirits of trauma as well. They need to 'eat.' They are always hungry. They create 'food' for themselves by generating more hurt. Why does the paradox exist, that victims of abuse become the worst abusers themselves? It is not logical, but it is perfectly reasonable for the spirits of trauma to grow in abuse victims through their hurts and feed themselves by *re-creating* those hurts. You may know this from your own experiences.

"How many of you did something in your life that you regret, that you knew wasn't the best thing to do, but still you chose to do it, bringing upon yourself unwanted circumstances? I bet you know the feeling. 'I don't have any idea why I did it.' I hear this often, and you probably do too from people you are working with. You don't have any idea because the impulse was initiated and supported by the spirit of trauma. You are not aware of it, so you follow it blindly and you end up hurting again and again.

"We practice a psychic science that recognizes the spirits of trauma and conquers them using very specific techniques. There are different spirits of trauma, relating to the age of the person and the quality of the trauma sustained. The justifiable next question would be, 'so what?'

"People adjust, they find their own means to cope, so why bother with looking deeper into it? Right?"

Some of the heads in the audience nodded in agreement.

"Wrong! Wrong questions. There are three main points for why it is vitally important for *everyone* to win in their battle with the spirits of trauma. First, because when you conquer them, it brings profound healing, reverses unhappiness, and treats disease. Diseases are the means by which an organism tries to fight the traumas on its own. So many times, I've seen people get sick and look for help at very particular points in their life, moments when the spirit of trauma becomes activated in a person with incomplete psychic memory. That is why many healing changes follow when you are able to eradicate the root of trauma.

"Second, we believe in our tradition that whatever we do directly touches generations before and after us. When you free yourself from trauma, you heal your ancestors and protect generations after you. I saw many people who would act out their traumas, essentially looking for help, when their children reach the age when they themselves experienced the hurt. Remember the man with his throat cut at the cemetery? His son was eleven. It was his chance to heal his family line, to save his ancestors and to protect his heirs. This was his chance to become the family hero."

"Question!" called out a voice from the audience. Vladimir turned to the voice and paused, waiting for the question. When I looked there, I recognized Phil. He was sitting on the floor near Victor. Phil seemed to be much more relaxed and happy than the first time I saw him.

"In the Native American tradition, there is a belief that our actions are responsible for the well-being of seven generations before us and seven generations after us. Do you think it is the same concept?"

"I don't think it is a concept," said Vladimir, and smiled for the first time. His smile was so direct and disarming that it immediately won over the audience. "It is not a 'concept.' It is a way of living your life, feeling its boundaries and borders. It relates to what you ultimately understand as 'self.' All knowledge comes to that understanding. But with any knowledge, the truth is that you can't obtain it just by making the decision to do so. You have to exchange your personal experience for it.

"All of you in this room have created the wealth of your experiences in your own unique ways. Yet it brought you here tonight so you will receive this knowledge. I believe that without those experiences that prepared you, you wouldn't have come tonight. Your car would have broken, your friend would have called, and so on. It is true for those who didn't plan to come but who happened to be here seemingly by accident. Believe me, it was not an accident, but your experiences which strive to become knowledge, that brought you here tonight."

I felt the familiar butterfly sensation in my abdomen as he finished that sentence.

"And seven is a very good number; my favorite, in fact. Thank you for bringing it in." Vladimir bowed his high turban toward Phil. When I looked to Phil's side, I noticed Smirnov standing near the wall behind the rows of seated people, his gaze fixed intently on Vladimir. His face was serious and concentrated, and it was clear that he accepted Vladimir as an eminent authority—something he wasn't used to doing. I remembered Masha's words and thought that she probably was right about his motivation.

"Third," Vladimir said, continuing his speech, "I am going to talk about death. It is not something many people like to talk about. Do you know why? There is a fear we all feel. They say it is fear of the unknown. I say it is fear of the *known*, but not realized consciously. When we go through life, the traumas we experience stay in us as painful knots, and are tightened by the spirits of trauma. If we don't untie these knots during our lives, we are going to have this done after our physical deaths. It doesn't matter if we believe in the afterlife or not.

"You may recall the abundant evidence that the experiences remembered from near-death experiences are just a reaction of brain activity fading away, playing tricks on the dying perception. Does it matter for you if those few objective minutes become eons spent in a subjective hell? I don't think it does.

"One thing you need to believe is that, with death, the experience of time changes radically. To enter death is, in a way, to enter time itself, and there you'd better be ready. There are many accounts of light and bliss, but this is only a beginning. What comes afterward is also described, but it is just not as well publicized. Angry, malicious spirits come next; they come to suck your blood and torture you by all possible means, but they are *your own* spirits of trauma. They will torture you until you untie the knots in your memory and become free. Again, it doesn't matter if you believe in the afterlife or not. I am talking about the subjective psychological process of restructuring your memory. Would it make a big difference for you to know that it all happens minutes after death, even though you may personally experience it as ages of torture?"

"Do you refer to the evil spirits from the Tibetan Book of the Dead?" a female voice asked from a back row.

Some people turned to look at her, but there was no particular curiosity in their looks. Somehow, Vladimir had created such an intimate atmosphere in the room that we all felt connected to one another. Any question would sound like a question from the group as a whole, so it didn't matter who was asking it.

"I don't refer to that book. You do. But since you did, I agree that this is the most widely known description of the spirits of trauma. It is a powerful book, but it was created inside a particular culture which is quite remote from your culture, and therefore from you personally, isn't it? Now I am going to make it more personal for you.

"Let's talk about your Russian culture. It is Christian, despite many years of advertised atheism. In Christian culture you have your own book of the dead; you just never thought you did. It is the book of Revelation, the Apocalypse, the Christian counterpart to the Tibetan Book of the Dead and the Egyptian Book of the Dead. It speaks about the same process, but in a different language. The Apocalypse is not a collective happening; it is profoundly individual. The seven seals it describes will be taken off each of you when the time comes, and then you will face the spirits of trauma of your lives.

"Many of you think that this subject is far from your actual interests. Many of you find yourselves attracted to magic, thinking that, in it, you may find powers and insights that will change your life once and forever. Who would think about death when there are so many exciting secrets that life can share with us?

"Well, people who are close to real magic would think about death and about what is beyond it, because they know that most of life's secrets come from mastering that space beyond death. The people who are known to have come closer than others to the realm of magic are the ancient Egyptians. They never fail to fascinate us. With amazing regularity they keep launching their archaic images into our modern consciousness, and our modern consciousness remains hypnotized by the power of their magic."

I looked to my left and saw Smirnov in the same place, transfixed near the wall. His focused eyes looked absolutely black contrasted by the unusual paleness of his face. Vladimir didn't look at Smirnov directly while talking, but I felt that he was well aware of the intensity of Smirnov's listening. It was almost as if an invisible but powerful exchange was happening between them while Vladimir was talking.

"When I talk about Egyptian magic, I know what I am talking about. Their knowledge came from the same experience as ours in Samarkand, only ours preceded theirs. Their knowledge was promoted through history while ours stayed hidden. But I know exactly what I am talking about. The universe of Egyptian magic had evolved around explaining the mystery of the main transition, that of leaving the physical body. One might think that is it, the end; but for the Egyptian mind, it only *started* there. The defining experiences of the afterlife and its battles for survival were the most important point of one's individual existence. Because the stakes were so high, one's very existence was in question.

"To make a long story short, to survive in the afterlife required that you be able to catch on to the barque of the sun god Ra. It goes every night through the space of Duat, which is another side of reality, before coming back to this world at the dawn. You must be able to stay unharmed there, and to pass all the night gates without being destroyed and swallowed by the gatekeepers. The gatekeepers were no fools. They knew their jobs. They were thirsty for your blood and hungry for your destruction.

"The only way to pass through their gates was to look at them in their disguised faces and say, 'I know you. I know your name.' You do this, then they have to let you through. You fail, they tear your limbs apart, suck your blood, tear your flesh. If you recognize their names, then you are saved from a second death, from annihilation, and your existence will continue. So what am I talking about?

"Any guesses yet? I expect that, at this point in my lecture, you will recognize who I am talking about. The spirits of trauma, of course, our psyches' creations, our representations of hurts and suffering which we have accumulated, and which we didn't have a chance to heal. So what can we do about all this?

"Well, we can become equipped. It is not a point of this presentation to introduce you to all the practical tools of healing the spirits of trauma. That is a next step; so your next experience must deliver you to that point of knowledge.

"The only thing I can tell you now is that we all have the space inside of us where the healing work can be done and is being done all the time for each of us—even though we are completely unaware of it. This space is the space of our dreams, created to protect and heal us from our traumas and their spirits. This is the territory of the origination of magic.

"That's why we are called the 'dream healers,' because we work inside the dream domain. We initiate changes and transformation through that work. We work with reintegration of memory in the dreams, and we leave no space for spirits of trauma to exist in the memory when it is healed. We teach how to become able to look in the faces of your traumas and say, 'I know you. I know your name,' so they won't destroy you. It takes years of intense practice to become efficient in this; that's why we consider it a psychic science. You may obtain many powerful qualities as you move along this road, but the main goal is the same: to be saved from the second death and to know how to be born again.

"We have existed unnoticed throughout the years, keeping our ancient connections with people from other regions. We don't need to become more well known to do what we have been doing for centuries. But! There is one 'but,' and it is exactly what brought me here tonight to talk to you.

"The purpose of my talk tonight is not only educational. It serves to make some of the aspects of our work known to Western culture. The reason is that the critical time has arrived. I told you that the unhealed traumatic experiences which gain status of their own and become spirits of trauma continue their existence throughout generations. If they are not healed, they build up, connect, accelerate, enforce and support each other, and become collective entities.

"In traditional cultures, rituals of transition are very important. Before going to another of life's stages, a person must go through a deep initiation ritual, one that basically cuts off all traumatic knots from the past and clears a path for the future. Modern civilization, as you call it, has lost all its psychological rituals. It doesn't have the means to clear its members of traumatic memories. Therefore, at some point, these accumulate on the collective level and become very dangerous. This dangerous time has come. It could become many times more dangerous now than in previous times, when world wars were induced by the accumulated spirits of traumas. The purpose of my visit is to tell you that there is a great danger for all the people on the planet, but there are effective means to overcome it.

"That is why I invite you to come to our place in Central Asia, to Samarkand, to learn about our practice. I know many of you in this room want to experience magic. And it is a great desire. To achieve it, you need to know what other people have experienced as magic. It is not enough just to accept that the focus of magic work is internal. There are many internal focuses. You have to have a map. You need to ask for it from people who have been using the map for ages. Ask us and we'll help you.

"You can find for yourself the magic you've been looking for. You can be healed from whatever you need to be healed. Then you can become healers for your people, and through that you can spread out healing changes to the rest of the world. Sounds like a decent task, doesn't it? You are already on your way to magic. Enter its space with our help. It is not that long a journey, after all. It's really within you."

Vladimir didn't seem to expect an answer. He looked at the woman in the first row and started talking to her. He spoke very quietly, so people in the audience couldn't hear what he was saying. Instead, they talked to one another. It looked like the end of the lecture, but no one rushed to leave. Instead, people were getting up from their seats, walking toward the others. A few groups formed inside the hall with people talking animatedly. I saw in Vladimir's face that this was exactly the ending he wanted to his lecture. Phil and Victor and a few other people were talking to him already, concentration on their faces, probably discussing practical details of their expedition to Samarkand.

I found Masha in the crowd and asked her, "So, are we going?"

She looked at me with flame in her eyes and said in the most enthusiastic tone possible, "I believe we *are* going."

"You'd better believe it, since you promised to take me home after the lecture," I responded.

Masha frowned then laughed loudly so a few people turned to us.

"We are going to Samarkand, I believe," Masha said.

"Well, you still have time to take me home tonight, don't you?"

"You still don't get it, right?" She looked at me with her sly, charming smile. "You and me and a few others—we go to Samarkand."

"Really? I don't think that I made a decision to go. Did I tell you I did?" I said.

"Not yet. Not yet. But I know we are going. I can see the future," said Masha.

I wanted to say to her the same ironic "please . . ." that worked well earlier to stop her from her communication games, but when I looked into her face, I saw that she was serious and excited. Suddenly, her serious face reminded me of her lying on the chairs in this same house a few weeks ago. That memory somehow made me feel very sad. I didn't feel anxious anymore; a profound sadness overcame me and I couldn't understand the reason for it or its meaning.

To leave the room, we had to go near Vladimir and a group of people surrounding him. He noticed me walking through and talked to me as if he was my old friend, "It was great that you could come today."

"Thank you. It was a wonderful lecture. I wish I could learn more about your practice." I said this as a polite excuse to leave the room.

"Really?" His smile was so disarming that it was impossible not to smile back. His smile lifted a weight off my heart, and it was only at that moment I realized how heavy the feeling was that I'd been carrying for a long time.

"You know what? Let me give you this." With a quick movement, Vladimir unwound from his wrist a string of dark, polished wooden beads.

"Take these with you. They will help." I felt that it was so sweet of him to do that. His smile was still keeping my heart light and he looked so firm in knowing his purpose that I took his gift without hesitancy, thanking him sincerely. I put it around my right wrist the way he wore it. I felt that it would help me, but where and when, I didn't know.

When I was going to ask Vladimir more questions, other people surrounded him and the crowd pushed me away. I saw Smirnov standing aside silently. He nodded to me and I nodded silently back. There was no need to talk. I felt that this evening made us closer to each other than the hours of previous discussion, as if Vladimir's sincere and powerful influence washed away all unnecessary pretending.

I found Masha and she drove me home, but she remained serious and gloomy throughout the trip. Since she made that remark about seeing the future, she looked as if somebody turned off the light inside her so that she was now freezing in her own terror. I couldn't decide if it was okay to ask her about that change since I barely knew her. But then, after another crazy turn she had made on a slippery road, I turned to her and asked, "When you work with Smirnov, is that what he asks you to do—see the future?"

"Maybe," she said, but her voice sounded different, more mechanical and irritated.

"What did you try to see in the future the first time I saw you in his house?"

Masha breathed heavily, overcoming her irritation with my questions and trying not to be rude.

"Nothing. He didn't ask me to see in the future."

She remained silent for some time. I didn't ask her any more questions, but then she said after a long, tense pause, "He asked me to see into the past. There were a few girls who disappeared in our city not long ago. He works occasionally for the criminal department. They pay him a lot of money to assist in crime cases, so he asked me to do that job. They suspected it to be a case of gang rape in which a group kidnaps a girl, rapes her, then kills her. I was looking into it."

"How?"

"There are ways to change your perception of time. I am good at it by nature, but Smirnov taught me some tricks. To find a girl you have to connect with her suffering. For that you have to know what it is to be raped. Then it is real association. You have to reconstruct your memory and then extend it to the other person's perception, so it becomes the bridge through which you can find a physical body. So far they have found one. There are about fifteen more missing. I still have a lot of work to do."

I felt nauseous. "Maybe her driving is too rough," I thought to myself. But this thought didn't work to free me from the overwhelming feeling of anxiety and sadness which originated somewhere deep in my mind, and it seemed were the reasons for my nausea that couldn't be relieved by any physical means. It felt as if my deep memory was making me sick physically.

"Why do you let him do it to you?" I asked Masha, without turning to her, and looking straight ahead at the snowy road.

"I try to help." Her voice sounded so distant, as if somebody else was answering my question.

"But you keep hurting yourself. There should be other ways to do it." I was trying to overcome her distance, but felt that I couldn't; she was so frozen and so far away. She drove silently for some time and I didn't repeat my question. Then suddenly she slowed down the car in the middle of the highway, looked at the rear-view mirror to make sure there were no cars behind us, and turned toward me. She looked straight at me and said with fire in her eyes, "It hurts anyway, no matter what I do. You have no idea. And I will do anything it takes to stop it. Anything." She pushed the gas pedal and the car raced over the icy road faster than before.

I was glad when she finally stopped in front of my apartment building.

"So did you make your decision yet?" She asked me before I left the car, but this time she asked it in a seemingly indifferent voice. She sat silently for a while and then added suddenly, with the same indifferent voice, "You know, I will go to that place only if you go."

I looked into her serious and sad eyes, the feeling from our conversation still in my body. But the only thing I could tell her at that moment was, "I don't know, Masha. I will think about it." Deep inside, I felt I already had made my decision, and the moment I realized that, my nausea subsided and I felt better.

Chapter 4

Everything was arranged as if it were a business trip. The tickets were bought through some organization offering a group discount. Apparently, Vladimir had left for Samarkand first, leaving us with detailed travel instructions and an address where we were supposed to arrive a few weeks later.

Before our departure to Samarkand, I was seeing Masha almost every other day. Since she didn't have any strict schedule and was often bored, she would pick me up from work and give me a ride to the center of the city, where we would stop at one of the coffeeshops and talk.

I learned a lot about her this way. I learned about her interests, her tastes, her friends, and enemies. She talked a lot about men, always in a funny tone, emphasizing how insignificant this or that man was in her life.

"I have never slept with a guy more than twice," she would say, and she would look around to make sure that, if somebody was sitting nearby, he would hear.

"Please . . ."

"Seriously. Maybe there were a few exceptions, but I don't remember them. Honestly, I don't." And she would burst into her animated laughing.

It was a part of her strategy, to talk about intimate details, often making them up, but to talk only on her terms, keeping up the impression of a superficial, naïve, reckless girl to create a sense of special trust that people could feel toward her. I understood this ploy, but I still enjoyed her company. Somehow her rules were easy for me to follow, and it was comfortable to pretend that I saw her reality in the light she wanted.

Only once, when I asked her, "And Smirnov? What about Smirnov?" did her face cloud immediately, and in the familiar mechanical voice, with evident irritation, she said, "What about him? I didn't sleep with him. There is no need to." Then she fell into a long, heavy silence, smoking one cigarette after another. I didn't ask her any more questions about him, but I knew he was not in the group going to Samarkand.

Everything was prepared for our flight. I wasn't sure how large our group would be, since Masha was the only person from the group I kept in contact with, and she didn't know. It seemed that a few people were considering going but would not be sure until the last moment.

We were supposed to leave late in the afternoon, to arrive at Samarkand at night after a stopover in Tashkent, which was a two-hour flight south from Novosibirsk. On the day of our departure, I packed my bags and called Masha in the morning to make sure she would pick me up to go to the airport. She sounded a little anxious, but assured me she would be in my place not later than four in the afternoon. Exactly at 4:00 P.M. my phone rang and an unfamiliar female voice asked if she could talk to Olga. When she learned that it was me, she introduced herself as Masha's grandmother, of whom I had never heard before. Masha kept telling me that she lived alone with two red cats, that her parents had died when she was young, and that she didn't have any family.

"No, her parents didn't die. They are just not here. But it is a long story," the woman said with some reservation in her voice, after I asked her.

"Masha doesn't live with me either. It is true. I live in an apartment next to her. I called you now because she asked me to do that before she fell asleep."

"What do you mean she fell asleep? Our flight is in a few hours!"

"She fell asleep because I gave her tranquilizers. She was drinking again—since this morning, trashing her apartment. The neighbors called me, so I had to come over and calm her down. She didn't tell you about her alcoholism?"

My head was spinning. I didn't know what to say or ask, but I surely knew that everything this woman was saying was true, as much as I wanted to believe differently. I was angry with Masha, but much more than that, I was angry with myself. I felt like I was now forced to face something I had made a lot of effort to avoid seeing. How could I possibly miss her drinking without unconsciously pretending not to see it? What was the advantage for me of refusing seeing it? And what was I supposed to do next?

"Let me talk to her."

"I told you she is asleep. She won't be able to say anything for at least a few hours."

"Wake her up, make her talk to me, or give me your address and I will come there myself!" I felt I was losing it.

"Okay. I'll try," the woman said with some irony.

The phone was silent for a while. I heard only distant muted sounds and then, suddenly, Masha's voice, deep and hoarse, burst into my ear as if she was sitting next to me, "So, doctor, I canceled my trip." Her slurred speech was difficult to understand.

I kept silent and was ready to cry.

"Did you hear what I said? I s . . . a . . . i . . . d I am going nowhere. You know why? Because I think it is much more honest to drink like a pig. . . ." She giggled and paused. "Instead of rushing to some hole in Asia just to escape myself, . . . doctor." The dial tone ended her ramble—she had hung up on me—but I kept holding the phone in my hands, paralyzed, not knowing what I was supposed to do.

The moment I replaced the phone, it rang again and the grandmother's voice, with blame in it, said:

"It took me a while to calm her down again. Do you want the address for your trip? I believe your flight is in a few hours."

I mechanically wrote down the address she dictated. I checked out my bags to make sure everything was in place. I called the cab to take me to the airport. I looked once more at my ticket to check the departure time. I did all that without thinking. My mind was totally blank, even though on the surface I was functioning well. Only when I took a seat on the plane, which was completely filled, did I realize what I was about to do. Masha was not sitting near me. She was drunk in her apartment, and I, sitting on that plane and feeling so upset with her, didn't know yet that on that morning, Smirnov had prohibited her from going to Samarkand and that she didn't dare to disobey him.

The more I looked around, the more anxious I became. Besides local passengers, there was a small group of European tourists sitting in a separated part of the plane. I was desperately looking around, trying to see familiar faces. No Victor, no Vladimir. And when I heard foreign tourists speaking German (there was no trace of Phil among them), I felt panicky. But it was too late. The plane was already in the air, and the vast space of the Siberian valley was falling steadily away from my view as the clouds surrounded the plane. I was on my way to an unfamiliar place all by myself. The only direction I had was a piece of paper with a Samarkand address. I didn't have any idea what to expect from this trip.

It wasn't the first time I had visited Uzbekistan. Fortunately, Tashkent and its airport were familiar to me. The exhaustion of flight finally overcame my distress, and I accepted the idea that I was on my way to Samarkand and that somehow, everything would become clear.

I started to feel anticipation about visiting this ancient city. Samarkand, one of the jewels of Uzbekistan, was closer to Novosibirsk in distance than Moscow. Yet it remained a mysterious and remote territory, and not many people would choose a trip to Uzbekistan over usual vacation spots such as the Black Sea or Moscow and Leningrad. The whole region of Uzbekistan was exotic and psychologically distant from Siberia. I knew it was one of a few places on Earth where all religious traditions had existed and influenced the culture. It was a home of ancient shamanic practice, of proto-Zoroastrian cults of Turan, and of Zoroastrian tradition. Later people in this land experienced Buddhism, Christianity, Judaism, practiced for ages by a strong community of Bukhara Jews. Even though modern-day Uzbekistan is largely a Muslim country, one could expect to find there marks of other traditions, and as I approached it, I started feeling more lucky than worried about my trip to Samarkand.

Once I arrived, the night air of Samarkand hit me with its aromas of flowers and freshly baked bread. Fields of tulips, impossible in Siberia this early in spring, flourished in abundance everywhere here, a city lit by electrical lamps to create an impression of being an exotic garden, hidden far away in a different space and time.

I called a cab. The driver immediately recognized the address I showed him, and that gave me confidence and calmed me down.

The drive was short, and because of the darkness I couldn't see much except the shadows of large branches of the trees planted along the streets. Behind them stood small, mostly one-floor adobe houses.

Suddenly, the road widened and we drove up to a large, tall building, its lights blazing and loud, modern music playing inside. Groups of people stood smoking and talking at its entrance.

I had expected to come to some type of a center, to meet a group representative or somebody who would be waiting for me at this address. I didn't expect the address to turn out to be the main hotel in Samarkand. Anxiously, I showed the address again to the driver, asking him to check that he hadn't made a mistake in taking me there. The driver showed me his printed map, indicating a hotel at this address, so the only thing left for me to do was to take my bags and get out.

I walked through the hotel lobby with fading hope of seeing Vladimir or somebody from the group. My intuition told me that this wasn't going to happen, and I had learned by that time to trust my intuition.

A young Uzbek girl who was the receptionist took my passport and cheerfully informed me that a reservation was made for me to have a room; otherwise, I would have had to find another place to stay since they were completely full. She pointed to where a few families were sitting on couches, surrounded by bags, looking desperate and exhausted, under a sign that said "No Rooms."

I guess I was supposed to feel privileged. I did feel relieved, even though there was no message for me at the front desk. Somehow my mind didn't fully register that the reservation had been made under my name at the hotel, and therefore somebody was aware of my coming here. I had a room, and at this hour, it was pretty much the only thing that counted. The room was small, warm, and cozy. I left my bags and remembered the loud music coming from the bar downstairs. The excitement of my travel was too strong to let me sleep and I decided to go to the bar, without hoping to find anybody from the group. Mostly, I wanted some rest.

I sat on the high wooden chair near the bar, trying not to turn my head and to remain unnoticed. The barman didn't make me wait for long. He sprang up in front of me as if from underground and asked what my order would be, but without saying a word. He just raised his thick, black Uzbek eyebrows.

"Just tea, please."

His left eyebrow rose for a second in surprise. People were drinking alcohol and no one was coming to the bar to order tea at that hour. But the next moment his face resumed his usual professional mask of indifference, and he faded away from my gaze. The next thing I noticed was a round, white clay cup covered with black lines of Uzbek design before me on the bar counter. I took a careful sip of the strong black tea. It was much too hot. I started drinking it slowly. To my surprise, every sip, instead of waking me up, was putting me into some kind of trance. The bar was crowded, and I couldn't recognize any phrases I heard spoken; everything blended into the background. The only objects I saw were the rows of colorful bottles in all possible shapes displayed on the bar wall. They seemed to sway slightly in accord with the music.

I watched the bottles, listening mindlessly to the music. For the first time in a few depressing weeks, I finally felt that, if not relaxation, at least the memory of it was returning slowly to my tense and exhausted body. This was what I desperately needed, and had been unconsciously looking for when I made the decision to come to this city in the heart of Central Asia. The touch of relaxation showed me how tired and unhappy I had felt all the time before coming here, even though I couldn't clearly see any particular reason for my unhappiness.

I didn't feel content with myself and with what I had been doing in my life lately. The sense of purpose that I had known so well before, and that was connected with my job as a doctor, had disappeared somewhere in my past, and I realized sadly how lost and confused I had been feeling for a long time. I was afraid to move, to scare this half-trance away, this half-sleep which I wanted to last forever and to carry me away into its mindless rest without people, without anxiety, and without the questions about this anxiety.

I felt gratitude toward this long-awaited relaxation, and thought to myself that maybe it wasn't such a foolish idea to come here after all. Perhaps I might be able to find a person here, a real person who, by a miracle, would help me out of my confusion. For some reason, I felt Vladimir was not going to play this role; that his main task of going out to other places and spreading the message about his tradition was already accomplished. I still hoped to find him here, but the anticipation of meeting somebody else, somebody who was connected with Vladimir and who stood behind him, was very strong.

Suddenly, I remembered the image of the small, aged, but dynamic figure of Umai, the Altai shaman I had known earlier in Siberia. A few years ago, she generated one of the most profound transformations in my life, helping me tremendously at that time, and since then, her image had become a prototype against which I would compare all subsequent meaningful encounters and experiences. Umai, in her shamanic outfit, a small drum in one hand and a lit pipe in the other, danced vividly through my mind. I saw her smiling face with its usual tricky expression as if she was near again, and this deepened my calm even more.

"Hi," said a voice to my left. I turned my head slowly, and somehow saw not the entire figure of the person speaking, but only his face. It appeared vividly against the vague, cloudy background of the bar—so real it looked as though it belonged to another dimension. It was a face of a very young man with thin, noble Uzbek features. He was extremely beautiful, with big, almond-shaped black eyes and such thick eyebrows they seemed pasted on his face, highlighting the intensity of his tender gaze.

His face was like a beautiful portrait—too perfect to be a regular human. I shook my head firmly, trying to restore my normal perception. It worked, and the next moment I saw a young man in a black T-shirt and blue jeans sitting on the bar chair near me.

He smiled kindly and was very shy. He was younger than I, probably in his mid-twenties. He now looked like the other locals who had come to the bar from the neighboring towns. But still, there was something different and special about him, some secret inside his deep black eyes. I tried not to pay too much attention to all this and politely said "hi," expecting our communication to be over. I was returning to my cup of tea and my fragile relaxation, when he moved his chair closer to mine and looked at me openly and cheerfully.

"You know, I am a healer too," he said, looking straight at me without blinking, playing with a blue straw in his hands. Then he put the straw into a glass and started to drink his cocktail slowly, looking at me from time to time with a smile.

"Aren't you too young to heal people?" I thought to myself, without saying it out loud, irritation passing through my mind. At the same time I had that thought I had a sense of inner confusion born out of my unexpected arrogance toward this inoffensive person.

He probably read my irritation and disbelief through the expression that briefly passed over my face. He smiled and repeated insistently, "I am a very good healer. As a matter of fact, I think, in all your attempts, you haven't come close to the hundredth part of what I know about healing."

That was rude and totally inappropriate. I looked at him more carefully, surprised by his behavior to such a degree that I didn't even register the fact that he knew about my profession and therefore knew something about me. He kept looking at me directly, but now his face lacked kindness. Now it was he who looked irritated by my inability to understand him immediately.

"And who do you think you are?" I dashed my remark into his face, almost short of breath from an unexpected anger that ruined all traces of my relaxation and brought my recent worries and troubles back to me afresh. I threw them out onto this strange man who by his bad luck happened to be near me at that moment, crossing a boundary he shouldn't.

"You must be some local spirit, no less," I added. I tried to accompany my verbal sarcasm with the most deprecatory expression my face was able to produce. I didn't know why his remark caused such a wild reaction in me, and it made me even more frustrated.

He placed his hand over mine on the bar counter, and before I had time to throw it off, a shocking thing happened, by which I was completely taken aback.

His face again became separated from the background. It grew so powerfully vivid that it completely subdued all other visual images for me. His Uzbek face floated in space in front of me with his eyes staring directly into my eyes and taking away my will. All sounds became muted and distant as if I were under some kind of anesthesia.

"What if he really is a spirit?" The thought jumped to the surface of my mind from somewhere deep inside. At the same time, it was as if somebody inside my head laughed at this thought. All this inner talk took place somewhere outside of my attention, which was now fully captivated by his black, almond-shaped eyes floating in front of me, putting me ever deeper into a hypnotic state.

Then I heard a clap, and as if by this mysterious command, his eyes grew bigger and bigger, finally joining to form one huge black eye in the middle of his forehead. This eye was looking at me and through me. It looked like a mosaic with diamond shapes constituting its inner structure.

Time stopped. He was a reflecting mirror that fixed my attention and made all possible movements useless and unnecessary. I had no motivation, no desire or intention after I met that gaze. It was a final destination, and even breathing didn't make much sense anymore.

Suddenly, I felt someone shaking my hand strongly. Then, following a recognition of my body's frantic attempts to breathe, I returned to my usual self-awareness. A cough was disrupting my lungs. My heart beat with unbelievable speed. He took his hand away from mine and gracefully moved the cup with my tea toward me. The tea was cold and had an unusual taste, but it helped me to stop my coughing almost immediately so I could talk.

"Who are you and why are you doing this to me?" My voice sounded strangely foreign to me, as if played from an outside recorder.

He was silently looking at me with a shy half-smile. But then, the next moment, he broke out in loud laughter after he reached out his hand toward mine, and I almost jumped off the chair instinctively, afraid he would touch me again.

"I know you," he said, still laughing, and firmly touched my hand again, but this time on the wrist, slowly moving his long fingers around my wrist over the beads that Vladimir gave me.

"What do you know about me?" While asking this question, I was trying hurriedly to put together different pieces of information to build up some reasonable picture of this strange encounter. But the picture kept falling apart.

"I know nothing about you. But I *know* you." His response did not help to uphold the rationality of the situation which was fast escaping me.

"I know you," he repeated. "And I think I know what you are looking for." He pronounced this last phrase simply and casually, without any trace of pretentious significance. But it struck me more than anything else that had happened.

I looked straight at his face with maximum concentration.

"Try to not look at me for too long," he said as plainly as if he was suggesting another cup of tea.

I looked at him with even more attention. It would be good news to my mental balance to find out he was crazy. It would easily explain all the oddness of his behavior. So I tried hard. I squeezed my eyes, and a list of all applicable diagnoses rushed through my mind, leaving me frustrated and disappointed. If I were sincere, I would have to admit what I knew already instinctively. This man, strange and weird as he was, had more sanity than most people I knew. Despite his request, I kept watching his face. He looked very young. At the same time, he somehow fit my expectation of someone who could manifest magic. In a way, he was a perfect candidate: secret, unpredictable, eternally young, and totally lonely.

I felt that the experience he had just generated through his influence was a result of some tremendous unknown power flowing through him.

"And why is that? Why do you advise me to look at you only for short moments?"

"It is only for a few days," he replied. "After that you will get used to being near me and that won't be necessary." He clearly didn't want to accept the irony of my question.

"And what makes you think that I will have those days to adjust to the power of your gaze?" I couldn't restrain myself.

"Because you have to first adjust before doing what you really came here for."

"And that would be . . . ?"

"You know better." He stood up from his chair abruptly, his face tired and somewhat disappointed. He took money out of his pocket and put it on the bar, following the barman with his eyes to make sure he noticed. One more moment and he would leave here without saying another word to me. Suddenly, I felt awful, as if I had hurt his feelings without even understanding what I had done wrong. All the unexpected emotions he caused in me showed me clearly how unbalanced I myself became and it felt bad. I wanted to say something agreeable to him, to end this conversation nicely, but my mind kept telling me that I couldn't allow this man to manipulate me any further.

He turned away and was about to leave, when suddenly he stopped for a moment, and returned to me with his nice half-smile. He touched my wrist again, reaching to the string of beads, and said, smiling even more nicely, "I like your *chetki*," he said about the string of beads I wore around my wrist. "Do you think you can give them to me?"

I reached for the polished beads and carefully, so as not to break the thin thread, pulled them off my hand. I didn't question what I was doing. I suddenly felt very tired from this encounter, and I wanted it to end—and end pleasantly.

I handed him the long beaded string, feeling at that moment that it was somehow my own safety I was giving him.

He put them gracefully around his neck and bowed his head slightly, thanking me.

"You may find me tomorrow noon in the *chaikhana*, the local tea place. It is very close by. You can walk from here. I will show you some things."

He quickly turned away and left the room without looking back.

Chapter 5

I was waiting in my room the whole morning. The phone kept torturing me with its silence and I didn't have any number to call to break the silence and stop the uncertainty.

At one point, my nervousness reached its extreme and I felt that I couldn't stand it any longer. It was exhausting to be in this small room waiting for God-knows-what. I needed fresh air. I needed to soothe my fear.

I don't remember exactly how I made the decision to go to the *chaikhana*. Maybe I talked myself into it, creating a rational reason for an irrational act. Maybe I followed an intuitive impulse to walk the hundred meters from the hotel to the small, one-floor mud house. The hotel clerk had pointed out the white-painted building as the local *chaikhana*.

I remember standing in the doorway before entering the small hall of the *chaikhana*. That memory, and the memory of all that happened later, is like an unusually vivid dream. The *chaikhana*'s tiny windows were half-covered with floral curtains, making the room dark and cozy. There were massive, wooden Uzbek tables with color-ful fabric pillows placed on the long dark benches; here visitors would sit and drink tea in the traditional way. A few old Uzbek men, in warm long robes tied around their waists, were seated around one of the tables, quietly talk-ing to one another. There were also a couple of modern plastic tables with light chairs nearby. This break with tra-dition probably was inspired by the frequent visits of hotel guests.

At this early afternoon hour, the tea room was almost empty. The guy I met yesterday was sitting on the chair at one of the modern tables, though he was looking away. As I walked closer, he slowly turned his head toward me and a smile lit up his face. He was wearing a white cotton shirt with long sleeves rolled up to his elbows. The shirt was unbuttoned to the middle of his chest and I could see Vladimir's *chetki* still hanging around his neck. The *chetki* made me remember the purpose of my being here and it gave me the confidence to make the few last steps to the table.

He stood up a little, then sat back down when I took my seat in front of him. His half-smile lingered, but his dark eyes were looking at me seriously.

"Hi," was his first word, and before I had time to reply he said, "You look strange today."

"Great," I heard my inner voice say, "the weirdest guy I've ever met tells me that I look strange."

I tried to remember the image of myself that I had seen this morning in the mirror at the hotel. Black, long-sleeved T-shirt, gray knit pants, a money belt, soft, local leather boots embroidered with a folk design, blond hair in a ponytail, a slightly tanned and tired face. Nothing strange.

He looked at me, concentrating on something. Then he looked around the room and I followed his gaze. Somehow

I could see that same hotel mirror image of myself in this strange place, surrounded by all the trappings of Uzbek culture, with faint music accompanying a male voice singing in an Uzbek language. At that moment, I understood immediately the man in front of me. The group of men in their warm quilted robes sitting on the carved benches, the exotic, captivating smells, the lullaby rhythm of the song, the unusual warmth of the air at this early hour—none of this was foreign. They were all in their own genuine places, where they belonged, and it was I who was foreign to everything here. I did indeed look strange because it was I who didn't belong here. Instead of making me feel uncomfortable, however, this realization made me feel more grounded. So I shook my head slightly and kept looking at him.

"I am Michael," he said, and took a sip of tea from a *piala,* a round, shallow teacup without a handle which he held carefully with both his hands. "And I know you are Olga," he said before I introduced myself.

The fact that he knew my name recalled the question that troubled me yesterday after he left the bar. How did he know about my profession? What else did he know about me? The most logical thing would be to ask him if he was connected to Vladimir and knew about me from him. But somehow I didn't feel like talking to him about Vladimir right away. It was almost as if my communication with Michael was developing in a realm different from my usual reality (or at least I wanted it to be so). I unconsciously resisted making a connection between Michael and Vladimir so as not to break the mystery. Looking back now, I believe that Michael himself was not interested in uncovering for me the nature of the link between himself and Vladimir. Rather, he was interested in increasing my anxiety and confusion to achieve his purpose, of which I was not yet aware.

"How much do you know about me, Michael?" I tried to ask in the most casual tone I could manage.

"Nothing, really, and at the same time almost every-thing."

"Do you want to explain what you mean?"

"No." His factual answer made it sound less rude, yet somehow frightening.

"And if I tell you that I would like you to explain it to me, can you?"

"I can, but it won't mean anything to you, because my explanations don't exist in that part of reality where illusory meanings are taken as the only value, and you would be waiting for an answer only from that part of reality."

"Can you give me *your* type of the answer?"

"Ask your question again."

"Tell me more please of what you know about me."

"First of all, I can tell you why you are eager to make sense of our meeting. You feel you don't have all the pieces of this picture and therefore you can't take it in as something comfortable and known. When you don't have all the pieces, you start feeling irritated, somewhat distressed, maybe even threatened. So you look for those missing parts to dissolve your anxiety and discomfort. But this is exactly the opposite of what you need. The anxiety and worry which you currently experience, and which grow in you right now as you listen to me, are your only hope to get out of your predicament. You don't need to dissolve your discomfort. You need to accelerate it and follow it."

I noticed how my leg crossed over the other was jerking rhythmically faster and faster while he talked. There was a sensation of a small, angry, catlike animal nervously turning inside me, behind my sternum, scratching me from inside and wanting to jump out to bite this man who caused this wave of irritation.

I took a deep breath and tried to overcome my uneasiness and continue listening without interruption. Again, I sensed that none of my reactions stayed hidden from his focused, penetrating eyes. Michael smiled slightly and kept talking.

"Good. You can get angry easy. It's good. You need to feel it even more. Because if you don't do it, the only other choice you have is to fall back to that dark, silent hole where you have been residing almost all the time before now. You ask me for meaning as you would for oxygen, so that you can take it and dive back into your deep, deep well, filled with your depression. The well surrounds you like a cloud on all sides, closes your eyes and ears, and numbs your feelings. As a result, you don't have to feel one basic truth anymore, one true feeling, and you try to bury it with all your games. This feeling is simple; it is called guilt. You wish to avoid feeling guilty."

The thin membrane holding in my anger couldn't hold it any longer. It blew up, my sight darkening from this amazing energy filling me. I jumped to my feet, breathing heavily. I glared at him as he sat in front of me with his hands holding the *piala,* and his relaxed, smiling face. I felt insulted and violated and overwhelmed by the unexpected intensity of my reactions that this man was causing in me. And I didn't know what to do next.

"Sit down," he said very calmly. "I have to tell you more."

I slowly sat on the edge of the chair and noticed how Michael made a gesture signaling to the *chaikhana's* cook, who was standing nearby pretending not to hear our conversation. The cook bowed his head, showing that he understood and went to the kitchen.

"Listen to me. I don't know the reason for your depression and your guilt. I don't look for meaning or content when I communicate with people. I see energy. I see how it flows, where it slows down, where it meets obstacles, where it starts going in circles creating the knots in the dynamics of your life—knots which can eventually kill you. When you give in to your depression, you betray your energy. You give it up, and there are always powers around who want to use it. If you refuse to explore it with me, the painful lump will solidify in you, and it will deprive you of the real gift which you have—the gift of healing. You won't be able to heal people anymore if you refuse to heal yourself. You've got to trust me."

His words sounded true. I felt calmer now. It was as if there were too many different impulses in me now. I didn't have enough strength to sort them out, and was inclining toward the least taxing choice of trusting him.

The cook, with his long, gray, quilted robe and a white linen apron around his huge belly, walked out of the kitchen with two deep plates filled with hot and amazingly fragrant *plov*, the native food of meat, rice, and herbs, cooked in a special kettle. He placed the first plate in front of Michael and the second one in front of me.

"Thank you, but I am not hungry," I said.

"This is my treat," the cook said in a low voice, and it was clear that he would consider it an insult if I refused to try his food.

"Thank you," I said again, and looked around in search of a fork and a knife.

"No, we eat it like this," said Michael, laughing and shaking his head.

He carefully put his long graceful fingers together as if he was preparing to play a musical instrument, and took a portion of rice and meat out of the plate. He held it for a second and then made a few slight movements firming up the rice under his fingertips and then put the ball in his mouth, obviously enjoying its aroma and taste.

I had to do the same. I stretched my hand toward the plate, picked the smallest and driest clump of rice, and when I placed it in my mouth, the warm aroma of this food filled my senses. I felt that I had never before experienced so intensely the sensation of eating.

Michael kept talking in a slow rhythm. "If you let this point of hurt crystallize in your memory as an unresolved knot, it will become an incubator, a womb to rejuvenate and to nourish a hungry evil spirit that has been waiting in your genetic memory line for many generations of your ancestors for this chance. It will rise up from the collective memory of your ancestors and start a life of its own as a spirit of fear. It will poison your life."

His mention of spirits of fear brought Vladimir's lecture in Novosibirsk back to me. Could it be possible that Michael was one of Vladimir's group? Excitement and hope overtook my other mixed emotions.

"I know a person. We met in Siberia. I came here because of him, and he gave me this address. His name is Vladimir. He told me about the spirits of trauma. Do you know him? Do you work with him?"

"I know no one by that name around here," he gave me his disappointing answer. Michael wasn't lying then. Vladimir's actual Uzbek name was different. He called himself Vladimir only while traveling in Russia, and no one called him Vladimir in Samarkand. But I, of course, didn't know any of that at the time, and I felt my anxiety accelerate as Michael continued talking. "And I don't think that you came here because of him. But don't jump ahead. Let me tell you more." The way he wrapped up the conversation about Vladimir didn't leave me a chance to get any leads from him. I sighed while he kept talking.

"Here is the situation. If you are unaware of the spirits of trauma, as you just called them, or memory demons, as I will call them, the best you can do as a healer is to provide a healing accidentally, without understanding what you are doing, or to render temporary relief which won't last long. If you want to heal for real, you have to learn what governs those spirits, you have to learn how to see them, how to hunt them, and how to become strong enough to win the fight with them. I can teach you all that. But I will ask you something in return."

He had a deep, low voice. It touched my feelings directly and I felt it encompass many different vibrations. The way he was talking, eating, looking around with his dark, intense eyes was extremely different from anything I had ever encountered before. He gave the impression of someone firmly grounded, full of earth-bound experience. The vital rhythm radiating from his body reminded me of the rhythm of Louisiana blues which I heard in a Novosibirsk nightclub. But, at the same time, I had a feeling I was talking to someone not from this planet, as if he were surrounded by a high cosmic vibration and it was signaling through him—except I couldn't understand the signals.

What can he possibly ask from me in return? I wondered.

"Healing." I was almost sure that he heard my unspoken question.

"In return I will ask you to participate in a healing ritual and to help someone who is in desperate need. It shouldn't be difficult for you."

"Okay. I can extend my stay here for a few days. Maybe I will find Vladimir, too."

Michael smiled somewhat wisely, as if somehow he had seen some cheating.

"Good. Let's start then. Let's go to the bazaar."

The suggestion was quite unexpected, but I knew that the Samarkand bazaar was near one of the main architectural treasures of the city, so I decided that it would be great to have a local guide. I gladly agreed to go.

It was a ten-minute walk from the *chaikhana* through the sunny green streets to the large, old town square where the bazaar was. Even from a distance, I could see the magnificent turquoise-blue domes of the Bibi Khanum mosque which long ago rose above its brown brick walls by the will of Timur, king of the "Mirror of the World," as Samarkand was called in his time. Timur was the Samarkand ruler known to the West as the fierce, lame tyrant Tamerlane.

I was walking closely behind Michael, who led me through the crowd on the way to the bazaar entrance. I tried to keep pace with his easy-moving figure so I wouldn't get lost. Even though I didn't stop to contemplate the Bibi Khanum's beauty, the radiating and alive power of its presence surrounded me. Its bright blue domes competed with the sky itself, and the fascinating legends surrounding its construction seemed to be not fantastic fairy tales anymore, but the real fabric of history merging with the power of the mosque's actual presence.

Khanum, Timur's favorite wife, the Chinese princess in one story or the daughter of the Mongol Khan in another, had decided to build this giant mosque to surprise her husband when he came back home from conquering India. A young Persian slave, the genius architect who built the mosque at Khanum's command, couldn't finish it, for he fell victim to Khanum's beauty. Only a royal kiss would give him the power to finish the mosque before Timur's return to Samarkand. The return of her husband was near, and there was only one arch needed to finish the monument, and there was only one kiss separating her from her goal, a kiss which Khanum finally allowed the architect. But the passion of his kiss left an indelible mark on Khanum's beautiful face, so that death in this very mosque from the hand of her wrathful husband became her final punishment.

As we entered the bazaar, a row of heavy oriental rugs hanging one behind the other caught my eye. Michael walked in front of me, parting the heavy rugs, clearing the way for me. The intricate designs of the rugs passed in front of me as though they were ancient veils, one after another opening up spaces hidden behind them. The sounds and the sights of the bazaar blended into one continuous noisy accord of clinking metal, chickens cackling in locked rusty cages, meat sizzling on huge frying pans. The pungent smell of herbs stuffed in colorful bags, the abundance of food, the hot air, the remote beat of a drum—all of it drew me ever deeper into this fascinating universe. I stopped following Michael with my eyes. Instead, I just walked through the rows of rugs and glowing fabrics, the seas of fruit, the cheerful faces. At one point, I saw Michael standing in an open space, waiting for me.

His face in the daylight, seen against the background of other faces, made him look different. He looked more European, as his features were leaner and had fewer Mongolian traces to them. I thought that he might be of Tajik blood as well. The descendants of Indo-European nomads who entered the territory of Samarkand thousands of years ago, Tajik people still preserved European features unmixed with Mongolian influence.

"You know the story of Bibi Khanum, don't you?" Michael didn't really ask me; he knew somehow that I knew the story, so he continued.

"It wasn't she who built it. Timur built it himself. But he built it not for his favorite wife, but for another purpose. He built it for balance. He knew that the only power that could be sustained through the ages was power in balance with the Earth. And he desperately wanted his power to be sustained. So he had to balance it. He had to work through the Earth with the spirits of trauma which he in his conquests had generated.

"But he wasn't the first. There were two others connected to Samarkand and to each other through the centuries: Alexander from Macedonia and Genghis Khan. Then Timur. This land became a battlefield not only for their soldiers but for their internal demons as well. In Samarkand, each of them underwent the main transformation which defined the fate of their afterlives. They experienced their demons in this land, and their histories were changed here."

After saying this, Michael fell silent and watched me.

"This is fascinating. Tell me more." I hardly could wait for him to continue his story.

"The main principle of balance lies in the ability to recognize the nature of the surroundings. Every place has its own determination. The home is a place to live. The battlefield is a place to fight. The mausoleum was built to serve its purpose to house the dead. We are now in the bazaar, and the bazaar is a place of trade. You can buy and sell here. But you can't tell stories here just like that. If you want me to tell you this story, you have to buy it from me. And because today is a great day for trade, I won't sell it cheap. But if you wait until we come to the place for telling the stories, I will tell you the whole story for free."

"I'll wait, I guess."

"I thought you would." Michael smiled again. "Let's go on further."

We kept moving through colorful rows of traders for another three hundred feet, when unexpectedly the bazaar ended and we stood in a large open square where a wandering circus was performing, surrounded by a crowd. Two large posts were firmly fixed in the ground with a thick tensed cable secured between them. Little platforms were moving slightly at the top of each post and on one of them, two people were waiting for the third, who was clambering up the post.

I didn't notice how the crowd moved me away from Michael, because my eyes were fixed on the dangerous preparation. The acrobats didn't have any security net and the construction of the posts and the cable fixed high above the ground looked too unstable to hold three adult men safely.

A few other circus artists on the ground were entertaining the public, making jokes in the native language, playing musical instruments, making announcements I couldn't understand. I felt transported to a long-forgotten childhood memory. It wasn't even a personal memory, for

I had never seen a wandering circus before. I just felt like a child myself, similar to the many excited kids around me who were impatiently waiting for the performance to start.

I looked at the adult faces around me. They all looked childlike too; even the wise Uzbek elders sitting in their low chairs smoking their pipes had genuine excitement behind their old, squinting eyes.

One middle-aged woman in a traditional striped silk dress waved to me from the other side of the crowd. She held a tambourine in her other hand and was striking it to the rhythm of the circus music. I smiled back at her, but she waved to me again, gesturing for me to come closer to her.

I approached her, wondering what she wanted. She bent down and took out a freshly baked, white disk of flatbread called *nun* from her bag. She handed it to me, and the moment she did so, its fresh smell so near, I understood that the aroma of fresh bread permeated the bazaar. This kind of bread was sold on every corner, and its inviting aroma filled the air.

I remembered the story of how Timur kept changing bakers, trying to find the one who would be able to make a bread equal to the *nun* made in his beloved Samarkand. Each would accompany him on his military journeys. Eventually he gave up, realizing that it wasn't the bakers, and it wasn't the flour that made a difference—it was the very air of Samarkand embodied in the bread that made it so unforgettably delicious. From that time forward, Timur ordered bread shipped to him directly from Samarkand wherever he traveled.

Now this woman of Samarkand was handing me beautiful white *nun* and I couldn't resist its fragrance or her smile.

"How much is it?" I was going to open my money belt to find some rubles, when she interrupted me abruptly.

"No! No! No money. The bread is a gift to you. You walk with *Chiltan*. *Chiltan* is in the bazaar. It is such a great day today. Such a great day for trade. You take it as a gift."

Confused, I took the *nun* from her, and a plastic bag to put it in.

"Thank you." But before I had time to ask her what she meant by saying that I walk with *Chiltan*, loud fanfares announced the beginning of the performance and every head was turned to the sky.

One man was standing on the cable, carrying a large, heavy pole in his hands for a balance. Small seats were attached to each end of the pole, and the two other men were sitting on them, moving up and down in their seats slightly as the ropewalker was making his first steps away from the support. The crowd froze. Kids stopped running, people stopped talking, only a little tambourine and a flute were playing in time with his steps. With their rhythm, he moved high above our heads, farther and farther away from the secure post. His steps were small, his burden looked very heavy, and he had the whole cable ahead of him to walk before he reached the other end and security.

He didn't hurry. I couldn't see his face or the faces of the men he carried. I saw only his relaxed back and his golden silk shirt and red *tubeteika*, a cap embroidered with an intricate design. From where I stood, the other post looked higher, so that, to my eyes, the walker was climbing, rising by small steps right to the sky, the same sky that competed with the turquoise domes of Bibi Khanum.

This acrobat knew his power. He knew exactly how much energy to invest in each step to be able to reach the other end of the cable. His steps were so precise and balanced that, at some point, I stopped feeling that he was in danger. He was a great acrobat. He knew how to walk the cable. But when I looked at the backs of the two others, who, in their identical golden shirts were sitting silently at the ends of the horizontal pole, I felt great fear again. And I felt that the whole crowd was mesmerized by those two who didn't have any way to protect themselves and had to trust the one who bore them. They couldn't see his movements. They were looking ahead, waiting to be carried on farther.

It took some time, because he moved slowly, but when he calmly and carefully reached the platform, I had the feeling that it was me whom he had carried safely across the cable up to the sky. The crowd burst into applause. The acrobats bent their heads silently, came quickly down the post, and leapt to the ground, one after another. I looked around. The woman with the tambourine was still nearby. I used the break in the performance to ask her.

"Excuse me, can you tell me please who *Chiltan* is?"

She looked at me with an expression of shock on her face, as if I had publicly pronounced myself insane.

"You walk with *Chiltan* and you don't know who he is?" She seemed not to believe her own words as she said them. "You are strange," was the only thing she was able to add.

That much I had already heard. I remembered Michael and thought that the woman's talk may have been connected to him. But I didn't have time to persuade her to tell me more, for I realized that I had lost Michael in the crowd. I started feverishly looking for him among the many faces. He wasn't anywhere around. I looked at and behind every face but still, I couldn't see him.

He probably left, I thought. He probably saw that I wasn't attentive enough to follow him and he left. I was surprised by the feeling of sadness those thoughts caused. The preparation for the next performance stirred a lot of excitement in the crowd, but it didn't interest me anymore. I felt sorry I had lost Michael.

The crowd started applauding wildly when another acrobat, a young man, almost still a boy, climbed up the stand. I looked to his side, and there, near the post, I saw Michael surrounded by circus artists and with a small boy in his arms. He looked at me, and I understood that he had been watching me all this time, never losing me from his sight. I smiled at him in relief and turned my head again up to the sky where the acrobat boy was already in the middle of the cable, dancing and jumping on it as easily as if he were on firm ground.

The music went wild. The performers were dancing on the ground along with the jumping figure of the boy in the sky who seemed to be flying above the cable, held by invisible hands. People were clapping and singing with the rhythm of the music and cheers filled the air. Then suddenly the music stopped. A whisper went through the crowd and then everyone fell silent. People were standing still with their heads tilted to the sky where the boy stood motionless on the cable, facing the crowd below with his eyes closed. A thin figure in a golden shirt and tight black pants, he was a sky picture on the bright blue background of Bibi Khanum's high domes.

He spread out his arms, opened his eyes, smiled at the crowd beneath him, and then effortlessly and gracefully pushed his feet off the cable and flew to the ground with his head down. The crowd gasped in one inhalation of terror. The boy's body flew through the cupolas, through the brick background of mosque walls, seemingly about to crash into the ground. At the very moment the top of the boy's head was about to hit the ground, his fall was stopped, and he hung in the air, suspended by long thin straps that were tied around his high leather boots. Hanging, he kept his arms spread out, flying up and down around the cable. His gold shirt sparkled in the sunlight as his body flew across the mosque's walls and cupolas, back and forth, like a lightweight brush held in the hands of an invisible painter. I walked through the excited crowd toward Michael. He had put the child down and was talking to the acrobats.

When I approached him, he looked at me and said without preface, "This is the discipline that teaches one how to transform space by using time as an ally. Our fears are contained in spaces that are arranged in certain ways so that we believe that they are indisputable realities. When they—" he moved his head slightly, gesturing to the acrobat-boy who had just jumped to the ground near us, "walk on the cable, their space is transformed. They don't believe at that moment that they live on the ground; they believe they inhabit the sky. They live in the sky and leap to the ground, coming to the place of the past from the future. They change the past of the people who are watching them by bringing the energy of the future from the sky."

"Why do you tell her all that?" It was the boy who asked this question as he gathered up his belongings. He obviously was irritated by my presence and by the conversation Michael was having with me.

"Because she needs to know," said Michael, his answer not an explanation but rather an order to avoid further questions. He not only knew all the circus artists but had authority among them. The boy bowed his head and quickly walked away. As much as I wanted to ask Michael questions to be sure I understood what he was saying, I had to postpone my questions and stand near him silently to avoid the growing irritation which I felt around me from the circus performers. They were gathering their belongings and a few of them walked by us and gave me unfriendly looks, even though no one said anything.

"We are going with them now. It is very close by. They need to show you something in their camp." This statement from Michael, when it was heard by the performers, caused a wave of tension among them. I saw how they walked aside in a group and started talking to one another in a whisper. The prospect of going somewhere with a group of angry men didn't enthuse me either. So when I saw two young women who came to me and Michael and said in a friendly voice, "Let's go to our camp," I was relieved and decided to go. My intuition told me that I would meet something important there.

About fifteen people, most of them men, left the bazaar and went through narrow streets toward their camp. The acrobats didn't change their golden robes, and were walking in front of the others and talking. I preferred to walk with the two young women, who were very chatty. Their dresses were different from the local, long striped robes most of the women wore. But their clothes didn't look modern either. They wore white blouses and long, flowing bright skirts, belted with leather belts to which were attached many white leather strips. Most of the people in this group wore similar belts around their waists.

We left the crowded part of the town, and in about ten minutes reached the outer part of the city. For a great distance, large open spaces lay in front of us, sandy hills and old, massive ruins extending to a horizon. A beautiful chain of connected mosques climbed a long hill to my right. A camp of a few felt tents was spread out near the ruins. Little children ran around ground fires, and large kettles with boiling food hung over some of the cook fires. A few old women, their chests covered by masses of gold jewelry, sat on low chairs smoking their pipes, looking at me attentively.

I felt uncomfortable. They didn't speak Russian and I couldn't understand the language they were speaking, which sounded like Uzbek. I felt a strong air of suspicion around me. Michael was the only person here whom I knew, but he was the most unpredictable of all.

"She needs to see the image," he told a group of men standing around him. They looked at me and didn't say a word. They just kept looking at me. The silence was becoming unbearable. To break this uncomfortable silence, I asked the first question which jumped into my mind.

"Is the image connected with *chiltans?*"

My question brought about a change I never could have anticipated. In a moment the men relaxed and nodded their heads, agreeing. I felt immediately their attitude toward me had changed, that the cold ice of their distance was replaced by the warmest welcome now radiating from them. One, the oldest one probably, opened up the corner of the tent, inviting me in.

I walked into the small space of the tent. It wasn't anyone's home, but a simple place, almost empty of household objects. A low, round table stood near one of the tent's walls with a thick lit candle stuck to a saucer on it. The candlelight was the source of illumination for this interior place except for a small tent window on the roof. In front of the entrance there was a large stone cube that obviously had been hewn because the evenness of its polished sides was almost perfect. Some large object covered by gray linen cloth rested on the cube. A man placed a chair in front of the stone.

"Sit down," said Michael's voice from behind me. When I tried to turn and look at him, he stopped me and put his hand on my right shoulder pushing me firmly toward the chair.

I sat on the chair and noticed how my legs were shaking slightly even though I felt surprisingly calm. The air in the tent was stifling and had a specific smell, as if a lot of herbs had been burned in this enclosed space.

"Close your eyes now," said Michael, who stood behind me, his hand still on my shoulder.

My eyelids became heavy and I closed my eyes.

"When I take my hand off your shoulder, open your eyes and look only straight ahead. Don't turn your head, whatever happens."

I kept my eyes closed. Michael's hand was still on my shoulder and I was waiting attentively for the moment when he would take it off to open my eyes. I waited a long time. The weight of his hand seemed so heavy that it seemed an eternity had passed, yet I still felt that weight. At some moment I stopped waiting. I stopped caring. I forgot all about his hand. Only when I felt my body become light, as light as if it were flying, did I open my eyes naturally and look at what was in front of me.

It was a stone face, looking at me. Its perfectly carved eyes were right in front of me, at the level of my eyes. Even though this face was carved in stone, it was somehow alive and communicating. I wanted to turn my head away but couldn't do it. My neck wouldn't listen to me. So I couldn't avoid this stone gaze penetrating into me, and I felt nausea rising.

The image dove into me, became inseparable from me, as if it was my own face. My nausea grew, my heart rate accelerated, and it was difficult to breathe. When these symptoms reached their climax, I realized with a shock that there were two identical faces looking at me. Two faces were carved on the stone, one above the other, and they were both deeply associated with me, as if this stone was a continuation of my body. The eyes of the upper face fixed on my eyes, while the second pair of eyes looked into my heart. The second face was carved below, in the place of the heart, and it was opening up my chest, pulling something out of my heart, causing a sense of unbearable pain mixed with deep sweetness.

"This is how magicians look at each other," said Michael, his voice as if it were coming into me through my chest, going through my body to the eyes of the second face.

"There are always two faces needed for any magic to be performed. Our city, Samarkand, was once called 'the Mirror of the World.' Most people think that this name comes from Timur's wish to build in this land the most beautiful buildings he ever met within his travels—to make Samarkand 'the Mirror of the World.' But there is another meaning to this name.

"Once, this city served as one of the two earthly faces mirroring each other in a special way. Samarkand was one face of this mirror. This mirror connection provided magic for the Earth for thousands of years, especially when it was much needed. Not much is known today about that connection, but once it was alive and powerful and many important things were realized through it.

"There were quiet times in history, but there were also wild ones. Through your coming here from the faraway north, it looks like the wild wave is coming again. So the work needs to be done again, the work through the second face, the face of death. And death is exactly what we need to work with next."

"Where is the second Earth face?" I was glad to feel that at least my voice still served me.

"In the place with the same name. In the country that mirrors us geographically. That country has also existed between two rivers as our country and with its people we share the territory of magic from the time unrecorded."

"The place with the same name?" I couldn't find an answer to what he said. My eyes fixed on the stone gaze in front of me; my mind felt powerless. Then things shifted, my awareness moved down to my chest, and I started looking through the eyes of my heart. With that, the easy and clear understanding raised in the space where my heart was connected to the second face of the sculpture. I received the thought "Sumer."

Of course, the same name, only with a slightly different pronunciation. Samarkand, in which the second part, *kand,* is a suffix meaning "city" has the same name as Sumer, whose territory existed between two rivers Tigris and Euphrates for thousands of years. I felt how the ancient mystery almost physically touched me.

"I guess you've had enough for today," said Michael, putting his hand on my right shoulder again. My eyes closed slowly, and when he took away his hand and I opened them, the stone sculpture was covered again by a linen cloth. I got up and walked outside to breathe the fresh air, and this quickly dissipated my nausea.

"Let me walk you to the bus station," said Michael as he came from the tent after me. And without giving me a chance to talk more to the people in the camp, he walked away. I said a quick good-bye to the men and women standing around and walked after Michael toward the bus station.

"Take this same bus tomorrow and come here at ten."

I asked him one more question. "These circus performers . . . they are Gypsies, aren't they? They are not Uzbek?"

"They are Uzbek Gypsies: *liuli*, the Dream Tribe. We go tomorrow to the place of telling stories, and I will tell you more there. Be here at ten."

Through the large back window of the bus which took me from this deserted area to the crowded center of the city, I could see Michael walking away. His slim figure was growing distant, but I saw he walked in the opposite direction from the Gypsy camp to the center of the deserted ruins and toward the long chain of cupolas on the other side of the hill. I knew I would be here at ten tomorrow, even though I didn't know on a rational level what Michael's purpose was in communicating with me.

I didn't know then that recently, Michael, Vladimir, and a few others had met here, on the ancient site of Afrasiab, at the remains of the old city near Samarkand, and made a decision to interact consciously with the West. I didn't know that after that meeting, Vladimir left for Novosibirsk, one of the Russian metaphysical centers, known for its unique combination of old occult traditions and advanced science, to look for the most suitable candidate to come here and to experience their work and to make it known to the West. I didn't have any idea that I was that candidate, that I was already inside the reality they prepared for me to go through or that there was no way back. I wasn't supposed to know any of that at that time, and I am glad I didn't know.

Instead, my awareness was focused intensely on my immediate experiences, which felt confusing and overwhelming, and I was trying to find a reason for my reactions. Michael definitely was an unusual person, but why did even his simplest remarks and actions make me so anxious and uneasy? I had dealt with unusual people before. I had the means to confront my deepest fears easily before. What was he showing me about myself that I was so desperately trying to avoid?

I felt that he had access to a hidden part of my memory that I was searching for and was simultaneously pushing away from my consciousness. I felt he had a key to that memory, and I didn't really have any choice but to be in this place tomorrow at ten. Then the bus made a turn and I couldn't see Michael anymore.

Chapter 6

Night had descended over the city when I walked into my hotel room. The Samarkand air, heavy and heated during the day, was gradually cooling. My room, small but looking nicer than before, didn't have an air conditioner, so I opened the window before going to bed. Sounds typical of a large city street filled my room: human voices, taxi klaxons, the sudden squeak of braking tires, the loud angry arguments that followed. As I listened to those sounds, they seemed so regular, so familiar, that they made me feel comfortable again. Even so, deep inside, a new feeling was growing and I knew it wouldn't go away.

It was a sense of being inside the mystery, the acute awareness of being presented physically with a mysterious realm of magic, in a city called the "Mirror of the World." This city was mirroring back to me the regular world I left far behind. It mirrored it as a remote illusion, and it was beginning to show me the sides of my reality which I hadn't seen reflected before.

But there was a danger in those sides of reality, I felt, and gradually behind the excitement and expectation, anxiety started to stir slowly in me again. The deeper I fell into sleep, the stronger it became. My whole body was like a boat floating in the waves of an unknown ocean. Then the moment came and a huge wave of dream came over me and took this boat of my body into its depth, cutting off all the safety lines.

I dove into the dream, trying to remember that whatever would happen to me now was only a dream and I didn't have to worry about anything, just to rest and to relax. The hot air of the room extended as if the room had become a cylinder, turning into a long tunnel connected to the spaces beyond the hotel wall. Surprisingly, I found myself flying easily through this space, leaving my room behind. I flew through the air, realizing that I was dreaming, but still aware of myself. Such dreams had happened to me before, but this time the quality of my movement was different, as if the speed of my body flying through the air was regulated by somebody's invisible hands. Somebody was holding my awareness inside the dream and helping me to keep the speed of my flight just right.

I recognized through this invisible influence that to keep my awareness and to keep flying, I had to maintain a precise speed. If I flew too slowly, the air wouldn't hold me and I would fall back asleep. If I flew too fast, the reality around would blow away and I would lose my awareness. One moment, I tried to look at my surroundings and my awareness weakened immediately and I almost lost it. The same invisible presence moved my focus back to my body and I realized that I had to make movements with my hands and with my sides to stay in flight. I did that and my focus reestablished itself, fed by bodily perception from all sides.

Suddenly, I saw the blue mountaintop. The colors of this vision were so bright that I had to make an effort to just perceive it without making comparisons and conclusions about this view. A huge, gorgeous eagle flew up from the ground as I approached the top. It flew in a circle, looking at me with almost human awareness. There were only spots of snow and ice on the brown ground. I didn't see any trees or houses. Nobody was there. Only the eagle continued flying in circles above my head as I stood on the ground. The inertia of the flight had pushed me to the edge of the cliff, and I saw a green valley with rivers and canyons far below. I was looking down from a tremendous height. The space that lay before me was open and inviting, and I still felt the drive to fly circulating through my body. But to continue flying, I had to jump into the abyss. I had to push my feet off the firm ground and let it go.

Fear crawled into my stomach from somewhere deep inside and stayed with me. I tried to overcome it and return to the ecstasy of flying, but now my body felt heavy. Now I felt I could crash. "This is just a dream," I said to myself, and that thought cut like a blade through my consciousness, separating it into right and left again, and I knew that now I would lose the whole experience.

The last thing I noticed before everything faded was the open lens of a small video camera fixed on a metal stand to my right. Turning toward it, I saw my face reflected on its surface as somebody else saw it on the other side of the camera. Something pulled me back, my dream disappeared, and I fell into a heavy sleep.

I was at the bus station thirty minutes before ten the next morning. I was the only passenger at that station, which was the end of the bus round, and the driver let me stay in the bus until the time of his scheduled departure. He was an Uzbek man in his late fifties, his face sharpened by exposure to the sun. His sad, wise eyes were those of a man who had worked too much in his life and received too little in material rewards. But he was a man who gained wisdom, which he kept secret, as to why life is so generous to some and so reserved to others.

"This place . . ." He made a wide gesture toward a chain of mosques, out on the edge of the ruins. "The ruins where the old city used to be are called Afrasiab. The mosque is called Shakh-i-Zendeh. We call it 'the Place of the Alive King.' There is a legend that long ago, inside those walls, the king was praying to God when suddenly the enemy army invaded his town and started to kill everybody. He made a choice, a strange one I must say, to continue his · prayers, even though his own life was now in danger. He was a devoted king. And, to nobody's surprise, the enemies killed him. With one stroke, they cut off his head and he dropped dead. So they thought.

"But because he was such a devoted king he didn't stop his prayers even confronted with the prospect of death. His god made him alive and placed the king somewhere underground, under this mosque, so he could continue to pray. People say that he is still alive underground and that sometimes you can ask him for something and he might make it happen."

"How long ago did all this happen?" I asked the driver.

"Oh . . . who knows? Legend is legend. Maybe centuries. Maybe thousands of years ago. No one knows."

"Which god did he pray to?"

"His main god, the one he believed in, I guess," the driver smiled cleverly as he lit his pipe and gazed contemplatively at the mosque.

I looked around but didn't see any signs of a Gypsy camp from the bus station. It wasn't clear to me if it was hidden behind one of the hills so I couldn't see it, or if the Gypsies had quickly left the area. Or maybe they didn't exist at all and everything that happened yesterday, including my meeting Michael, was a strange dream that had now dissolved. This thought, even though a joking one, was irritating, so I dismissed it.

"Be careful," the driver said to me. I got the feeling that he willingly prolonged his stay at this empty bus station to make sure that the meeting I was expecting would be a safe one. I guess this middle-aged Uzbek felt some responsibility for a foreign woman visiting a deserted neighborhood at that early hour.

"Hi." I heard Michael's voice from behind. I was looking to the side of the mosque where he had disappeared yesterday, expecting him to come from there, but he unexpectedly approached from the opposite direction.

"Well, have a good day," the driver said, quickly taking his seat in the bus, as if he was reassured that my meeting was safe and he could now leave. I had noticed surprise on his otherwise self-controlled face the minute he saw Michael.

"Hi. I've been waiting for you for quite some time now," I said. I didn't have any idea why I said that since I knew he wasn't late.

"You wanted to come earlier. I guess waiting means something for you, doesn't it?" Michael said. He looked older today. He was still a young man, but his appearance didn't have the youthful vibration that had filled him yesterday. He looked as if he had prepared himself for some important job. His black hair fell loosely over his shoulders. He wore a kind of suit, though not a formal one, consisting of wide pants and an oversized jacket made from heavy black linen; he wore a white tee shirt underneath it.

I didn't feel like asking him questions. Michael's presence made me feel comfortable and secure, and his remarks reduced the fuel that fed my constant analyzing.

Without speaking, we started to walk slowly toward the side of the hill. The morning landscape had a surreal quality to it. The soft waves of the brown hills with the ruined foundations of the ancient buildings of Afrasiab between them were framed against the industrial city with its exhaust towers and high-rise buildings. It was very silent there. I walked over the ground which was covered with soft dust, and I imagined that this dust could have been lying there unbroken for thousands of years.

Michael's movements were decisive, yet graceful. His movements had an animal-like nature, like a pitiless tiger who knows how to gently conserve its power as it walks quickly up and down the hills.

"How did you sleep last night?" Michael finally broke the silence with his question.

"Good. Thank you." I didn't know what else to say.

"And how did you like the circus performance yesterday?" he asked next while moving up the hill.

"I found it exciting. It is amazing that they could do it without any safety net. Don't they feel afraid?"

"You can't walk the cable if you feel afraid." Michael reached the top of the hill and stopped there for a moment. This site offered a good perspective of the ruins of Afrasiab. On different levels among the hills, the squared foundations of ruined buildings lay in front of us. They felt more revealing than any complete building could be. Their abandoned walls at ground level opened up all the entrances and former rooms for observation, and there were no walls to protect the privacy of their spaces. Even though there had been no inhabitants inside these walls for ages, I still had a feeling of entering somebody's space that had become exposed forcefully when the buildings were destroyed in battles.

"Yesterday's performance was one of my favorites," Michael said, turning toward me and looking straight into my eyes, without blinking. "When I watch them walk the cable like that, I remember that the way they do it is close to the way we organize our life experiences. And they do it consciously. This is why I told you that the acrobats practice a particular discipline. There is a whole philosophy behind their actions, and after they accept it, it becomes the best safety net they can get. They can't fall off the cable unless they experience fear. This is true of all three of them, the ones who sit on the sides and the one who carries them across. All three have to be fearless. In the same way, our awareness has to be organized to achieve its potential. Right and left sides of the brain have to be balanced and silent when necessary to be carried across to another side of experience by the one in the middle."

"When you use the image of acrobats as a metaphor for brain work, what is the third one, the one who walks the cable?" I felt that Michael was close to telling me something very important.

"You are the scientist. You should know better. My guess is that it is the one who is responsible for balancing the spaces." Michael looked at me with no trace of irony in his eyes, and his response prompted me to think more about what he was saying. I covered my eyes with my hands to help myself think, and stood with my face covered for a while with thoughts flashing through my head. Of course he was right. Probably without knowing it, Michael had just given me a key that finally brought together many of my previous thoughts and ideas.

The limit of the asymmetry between the functions of the right and left hemispheres was now overcome by the presence of a third agent, the one able to coordinate their relationship and communication. I thought about the brain's anatomy and of one particular structure that has fascinated me since medical school. Suddenly, this structure gained huge significance: the cerebellum. A large part of the brain that contains the most neuronal connections, yet it is considered by medical science to be only a substrate responsible for the coordination of bodily movement.

I took my hands off my face, breathed deeply, and almost laughed from happiness when Michael's metaphor put everything in place. Of course, the cerebellum is responsible for external movements and is involved in the organization of internal spaces as well. And that includes spaces of imagination, spaces of dreams, spaces of memory. I remembered whirling dervishes who would spin for hours to generate an alternate state of consciousness. They definitely knew how to work their cerebellum.

Michael was looking at me with a subtle smile, waiting for me to complete my thinking. When he saw me looking back at him, he squatted and put a thin rope on the ground in a straight line.

"Try to walk this as if it were a cable in the sky. Try to imagine that you are yesterday's acrobats and now you have to walk this cable."

It sounded silly and I laughed. He laughed with me but gestured his head toward the rope, pushing me to accept his game. I put my right foot on the rope and didn't feel the rope's structure, it was so soft and flexible. I opened my arms wide and imagined that I held in my hands a pole with two heavy seats attached to it. I took a step with my left foot, putting it in front of the right one on the rope. Suddenly, I lost my balance. I had to swing my body from right to left to regain balance. Now I stood straight with both my feet on the rope and was afraid to take another step.

Parallel thoughts went through my mind. I was telling myself that this was just a rope on the ground and that I couldn't fall anywhere. At the same time, I tried to keep the image of the pole with heavy seats in my hands as if I were really going to carry them across the cable. I also remembered that Michael was watching me, and I felt silly that I couldn't take another step.

Finally, I pushed myself to take the next step and all my thoughts rushed through my mind, back and forth between inner talk and images, between the right and left sides of my brain. My body had to compensate for this intensity by losing its balance again. I felt I couldn't stand straight or walk straight across this imaginary cable. I had to pause for a while as my body regained its balance. Then, without thinking, I simply moved my awareness to the back of my head, to the location of the cerebellum, and tried to experience it as a center of my consciousness. Then a fascinating thing happened to my perception.

The moment I was able to identify myself with this focus in the cerebellum, an impulse for action rose in me as if I had found an engine waiting for me to turn it on. I felt a strong push from the back of my head and it pushed my body forward without thinking. Now it was difficult to hold my body back from walking ahead. I walked easily across the rest of the rope, keeping my arms open. My movements were so exact and easy that I understood how it could be possible to walk the cable high in the sky and not to be afraid. I jumped off the rope, took it from the ground and gave it back to Michael, who watched me with delight.

"You got it," he said cheerfully. I knew that he understood in detail what kind of internal process I went through to accomplish his task. The impulse for movement continued in me, and it was easy to walk through the ruins of Afrasiab as I followed Michael, who moved on ahead while he kept talking.

"When you are able to gain understanding in your direct experience, it always looks so easy that it is funny you could not see it before." I just nodded my head silently, for I agreed with him.

"That's why I think, Olga, it will be easier for you now, after you have experienced the difference between pure movement and movement complicated by memory burden, to understand our approach. In pure movements, all the energy you need is free and available to you. In complicated movements you have to carry, along with your body, a huge weight of mental constructs. That's why some experiences are very difficult to complete. They keep coming back to you because you can't accomplish the movement since you have too much memory weight attached to them.

"In the case of a traumatic experience which generated a memory demon, it becomes an active obstacle, not simply an awful weight. It becomes a strange force in your body that actively opposes you as you go through the experience and attempt to complete it. This force lives inside you and generates painful circumstances again and again. You are bound to run in circles around this pain instead of walking away and leaving it far behind. It is almost as if another self lived inside you, of which you are not aware."

I listened to him carefully. It was easy to follow him. But Michael's last remark suddenly reminded me of Smirnov's lab, of the computer screen with the pulsating stars, and of Masha going through those experiences. What was she seeing and feeling then? Why were there several selves registered in her experience? Suddenly, I felt very sad and I didn't know why. I didn't know, of course, that almost at the same moment when I was talking with Michael in Afrasiab, Masha was put into restraints in her apartment. Exhausted and sedated after a drinking bout that did nothing to stop her agitation, she was rushed to the psychiatric hospital to become an involuntary patient on my female floor.

"You feel sad now," said Michael, looking at me. "Do you know why?"

"No, I really don't. And you know, Michael, I feel very unusual these days. I feel unbalanced with all these emotions coming to me from nowhere. I usually have much better control and understanding of myself, and it bothers me that I don't understand what is going on with me now."

He stopped walking and looked at me attentively. Then he said in a calm voice, "This is exactly what you *need* to go through. I told you that yesterday. This is your only chance. You have to trust me and go through it. You are already here. You made your trip. Now you have to accelerate your anxiety and depression to complete them and be healed from them. Your feelings show that you have started real movement through your memory spaces, to use the analogy of movement for the processing of recorded experiences. Now tell me, why did you feel depressed now? What did you remember?"

"Nothing important. Just a couple of images."

"Listen to me, Olga. There are no important or unimportant images in our mind. Their importance is conditional and they are created by our minds, often to mislead us. The image is the key to a certain space of your memory that is always connected to another space. We contain memory spaces inside of us in the same way your Russian *matreshka* doll contains many small dolls inside one another, embedded within one big doll. There may be spaces inside you infected with a memory demon that has learned to hide itself behind different images in your memory to keep hurting you. So what did you see?"

"I saw a computer screen from one of the labs I recently visited. It had a map of the brain activity of one of the girls working in the lab."

"So did seeing a computer screen make you feel sad?"

"No." I was sure in my answer.

"Then what did make you feel sad? What image?"

"It was the girl." I felt I was almost ready to cry; Masha's image made me feel so sad.

"Are you friends? How long have you known her?"

"I've known her for a short time. She was going to come here with me but then . . . she just couldn't make it."

Michael was looking at me very intently while I was answering his questions.

"You are not sad about this girl, Olga. And you know that. She is one of the superficial covers which connects you with the space of hurt. There is something in her that serves as a key to that space in your memory where your sadness originates, but it is not her you feel sad about."

Suddenly, his remark caused a wave of anxiety inside me. It rose up and covered my sadness quickly and now I felt irritated with Michael and with his attempts to analyze me. I saw that the change in my mood didn't stay hidden from his attention.

"There are two basic ways we can react to trauma." Michael continued talking without paying attention to my anxiety, and it calmed me down somewhat. "They are often experienced together but, in fact, they represent opposite processes. They are depression and anxiety. There are two different types of memory demons standing behind these feelings, and they require two different types of healing.

"When you experience these feelings, depression and anxiety together, one of them is always primary and it is very important to recognize which one. In your case, the anxiety that you have been experiencing lately is your attempt to find healing for something that makes you very sad. The anxiety is your ally now since it keeps you alert and attentive to what is going on inside.

"The reason these feelings represent different processes is that the origin of their creation is different. We have two basic psychological processes which constitute all our experiences. Every experience we have is composed from action and perception. When I say action, I mean not only physical movements but internal movement as well—thoughts, ideas, intentions. Perception is external and internal as well. These two processes interact with each other all the time, creating our unique experiences through their combinations. When we are hurt, one of these processes suffers the most. When our perception is hurt, we feel anxious. It is connected much with how we are perceived by others and with whatever harm other people do to us. Depression results from hurtful action and it develops because of our imaginary or real actions or inactions that we believe were wrong.

"It is simple to describe it, but if you pay attention to this you will understand how these processes interact. You have just experienced what a pure action is. And soon after that your sadness came back. I can tell you right now that whatever hurt you keep in your memory is caused by your belief that something you have done or haven't done was wrong, and you feel guilty about it."

"But one of the main feelings I have now, Michael, is feeling irritated with you and being quite anxious because of all this." I was trying to be honest with him.

"And it is exactly right," he responded. You feel anxious and irritated now because I am influencing your perception to bring to it something you try to forget. My questions lead to healing. The real thing is your sadness and guilt."

I didn't feel like talking at that point. I felt there was much truth in his words. I also felt that I could have argued with many of his points. But at the same time, I expected that he would defeat my arguments easily and I would end up in exactly the same situation he wanted me to be—facing my unclear, disturbing feelings and trying to avoid them.

Since we had reached the top of the hill, I felt that I wanted to take a little break before walking any farther. The ground was dry and warm from the sun, and I sat on last year's yellow grass and looked straight out to the open valley below the hill we were on.

Michael sat near me and looked straight ahead for a while. Then he said to me in a very soft, soothing voice, "You have just experienced what a pure action can be. You can try now to experience what pure perception is. For that, you need to close your eyes."

As he said that, my lids moved down even before I made a decision to follow his commands. I thought to myself that I should be careful about giving him so much influence over me. But he continued talking in a soothing voice and my alarm eased.

"You need to do almost the same thing you did with moving across the cable. You need to make an effort to change your experience of self. Remember the acrobats? You are trapped if you are the one on the seat and somebody carries you through the height.

"You are in control when *you* walk the cable. They are different people. You can't jump from the seat to the cable. You just needed to experience the other person in you, the one who walks the cable. You did it well. Now you need to experience the perceiver. Move your attention, not to the back of your head as you did with walking the cable, but closer to your face. The level of your eyes is where your perception is centered, and if you try to focus your attention on that level and do not allow it to jump back inside your head, you may experience pure perception and you won't get lost in the spaces of your memories. Try it."

I sat with my eyes closed and noticed how many thoughts, associations, and questions were coming to the surface of my consciousness from the center of my head. I made an effort and moved my attention to my face, feeling the level of my eyes strongly and intently. When I was able to hold that focus, I suddenly experienced myself as a self quite different from my usual awareness. I was the watcher, the being who lives in my eyes always. I was aware of all my surroundings and perceived everything as clearly as if my eyes were open and saw everything around. There was nothing hidden from my perception.

"Good, you are very good," I heard Michael saying, but my reaction to his words shattered the balance. I fell back into my usual self-awareness. I opened my eyes and looked at the valley in front of me. It looked almost as if my vision had greatly improved. I noticed a herd of sheep on the hill far away, but now I could almost perceive the smallest details of their gray, fat bodies walking stolidly through the grass. It was as if my eyes were the lens of a video camera that had been suddenly adjusted after years of malfunctioning and I could now perceive everything clearly.

"When you experience sadness, it is a sure indication that the trauma is based on the fact that your action or inaction was hurtful. To start recovering from it, you need to activate the opposite process. You need to heal that memory by working with perception. Now try to reconstruct your sadness one more time."

I remained sitting on the ground, watching the valley in front of me. The landscape was so peaceful and my mind felt so calm after I experienced the perceiver in me that I couldn't find any response to his request. I couldn't feel sad anymore, even though I tried. I closed my eyes and tried to restore the feeling of sadness, but it wasn't coming back. Then Michael said to me, "Use the image of that girl as a key to open up that space. Remember her first to remember your sadness."

Masha's animated, beautiful face appeared in front of my closed eyes. I remembered her sitting in my office trying to persuade me to go with her to Vladimir's lecture. I felt a warm wave inside of me connected with that memory. I felt that I didn't feel angry with her anymore, but instead her image made me smile. I was smiling with my eyes closed, and then I heard Michael saying in a soft voice, "Try to remember this girl in different circumstances. What did she have to do with the computers? Is she in the same room with them? Does she have a choice in that room to do whatever she wants? Can she leave there any time or must she stay there until she is allowed to leave? What is going on with her there?"

His questions regenerated anxiety in me. The focus of my memory switched from my office to the computer room in Smirnov's house. I imagined Masha lying in a trance on the black couch with cords placed on her body, recording her every internal and external move. She is deeply in trance. She can't move her eyelids. Her body is paralyzed but her mind is active. Her perception is heightened and her memory is taking her inevitably back to that place and time where her body knows how it feels to be raped.

Tears gathered under my closed lids and the feeling of sadness returned to me and overwhelmed me. I was afraid to open my eyes and let the tears out.

"Now," I heard Michael's soft voice say, "keep this feeling of sadness in your heart and try to move your awareness to the level of your eyes. Leave the space of your memory where you can see the girl and become the perceiver again."

I felt that it was easy for me to follow his commands. I made an effort and I became once again a being localized in my eyes, the being which perceives everything. The feeling of sadness abated, but before it disappeared completely, Michael's voice prompted it to stay. "Don't let the sadness go away now. Be a watcher *and* feel this sad feeling in your heart simultaneously. Notice it there and continue to perceive it along with all the other perceptions, but without falling back into it."

I felt how his words were directly reshaping my internal moves. He helped me to stay focused and maintain this simultaneous experience. Both the experience and my awareness of Michael's presence intensified. I felt his influence now without hearing him, without looking at him. A feeling of sadness rose gradually from my heart into my chest, filling my chest and making it difficult to breathe. I was registering it as it rose. My head moved down as if I was looking at the ground. My eyes were still closed. And at the moment when the sadness filled my perception, I saw the ground (without opening my eyes) and saw its dusty and rough surface. The thin yellow blades of last year's grass hit my face and I felt the pain as if I had been thrown to the ground.

I moaned. The images of dusty dry ground filled my vision and froze in front of my closed eyes. It was as unmoving as a stone wall. I couldn't avoid seeing it. I knew that my pose didn't change. I was still sitting on the ground with my eyes closed. But the picture that now held the focus of my vision caused an incredible pain. I felt pain in my hands; they burned from hurt, and I felt pain in my lips as they tasted the salt blood from my tongue, blood that mixed with my tears.

"What do you see now?" I heard Michael's voice very close.

My lips moved very slowly as I answered him, "I have a vivid memory now. It's a very remote memory from my childhood. I was maybe five years old then, but I remember it so clearly now." I grew silent as the memory continued to flood me.

I continued to see the ground move in front of my closed eyes as somebody's hands were trying to help me. My body felt heavy as I tried to push myself to the ground, to glue myself to the earth and to not be lifted up. I could see the earth's surface in front of my eyes in unusual detail. I could clearly see the surface of every single stone near my eyes. I wished I could turn myself into one of those grains and get lost under the grass so nobody would find me and bring me back to this cruel world.

"Oh my God, Olga. It was just a cat. You can't react like that." I hear my grandmother's voice. My body becomes soft from weakness, my muscles can't resist anymore; my grandmother's hands pull me up from the ground. I cover my eyes with my hands because there are people around me. I feel how they look at me and I don't want to see their faces. I keep walking with my eyes covered as my grandmother takes me inside the house.

Now I feel I can talk to Michael.

"I was five years old and spent summer months at my grandmother's house in a small town called Kursk in central Russia. The house had a garden. There were flowers and raspberry and gooseberry bushes growing near the fence. There was a river a few hundred yards away from the house with a dark, thick forest on its other bank. I loved everything about that place. It was alive and magical.

"Our neighbors had chickens, everybody had a dog, and I had a cat. It was a black male cat with a white chest. It was big and shiny and it was so independent. He was a 'person' in my world, and I was the only one he related to. He would usually come home from his night of wandering and eat his food and then go away again, sometimes for a few days.

"Some of our neighbors who went to the other side of the river to pick mushrooms in the forest sometimes saw our cat miles from our home, running among the bushes, but he always came back. I never worried about him. I knew he had magical powers and he would always protect himself. I was the only one he ever allowed to pet him. He understood my words as I talked to him, and he made me feel that he was talking back to me without words. He was my friend, my confidant, my connection with magic. I wasn't worried about him when the neighbors came to our house and complained to my grandmother that our 'horrible' cat stole their chickens and ate them. It had happened before and I knew it would happen again.

"He was a wild animal. He had to hunt. The neighbors tried to protect their chickens, but he always outsmarted them, and the neighbors grew more and more angry with the cat. They would come to my grandmother and complain about the cat as if he was a dangerous criminal. I felt that he was almost laughing at them in his own cat's manner, and he continued hunting their chickens. On a few occasions, my grandmother agreed to give him away.

The neighbors put him in a car and drove him miles away from our home to the other side of the forest. A few days later another chicken disappeared from the neighbor's henhouse and I knew that my cat was back. I put a saucer with milk under a lilac tree near the house. The milk disappeared the next morning and in the evening the cat came to my secret spot in the garden and let me pet him. This process was repeated a few times. The neighbors would drive him away and he would come back. Sometimes it would take a few days, sometimes more than a week. But he always came back. I didn't worry about him.

"I didn't have any hard feelings for my grandmother's allowing the neighbors to take him away because I understood that he was a wild one. My grandmother had to do something to keep our neighbors calm. One time he disappeared for a long time. I waited for him every day and night but he wasn't coming back. I felt sad but I thought that even if he chose to live in the forest and not come back it was his choice. He was a free being. However, I kept putting a small saucer with milk under the lilac tree every night.

"One morning, a neighboring woman, the one who really hated the cat, saw me taking the milk away in the morning. She stood on another side of the fence separating our houses, her hands placed on her hips as she shouted to me across the fence, 'Who do you feed with this milk every day?'

"'My cat.' I didn't feel that I had to hide it from her.

"'You don't have a cat.' She was enjoying this conversation so much that she was laughing.

"'I do. He will be back,' I insisted, because I knew it was true.

"'Oh, really? You don't mean that black warlock your grandmother used to have, do you?' She moved closer to the fence to see my face as she was talking.

"'He will be back,' I kept saying, trying hard not to cry in front of her because I felt that was exactly what she wanted to see.

"'No, it won't. It won't be back, maybe only in your dreams, dear. Ivan, tell her what you did to their cat,' she shouted to her husband.

"Her husband walked out of the henhouse and paused on the doorstep, trying to think what she was asking about. After some time, he finally got her question, then he laughed with pleasure and answered her in a loud voice, 'That bastard? I cut it in half with this very ax.' He showed me an iron ax he used to cut off chicken's heads. 'I caught it and cut it in half and threw it into the garbage.'

"I remember how the milk was slowly spilling to the ground as my hand couldn't hold the saucer. I heard my own voice screaming 'No!' from a distance. Then I remember running in slow motion, as if in a dream, through the narrow trail going toward the house, tall grass and bushes on its sides. My legs felt like cotton. I was trying to run faster but my legs didn't obey me. A bush's long branch blocked my way; my feet got caught in it and I flew to the ground with my face down. My hands burned from the injury. My lips tasted the salty blood of my bit tongue. The dusty, rough surface of the ground with last year's grass, thin and yellow, hit my face, and I wanted never to be taken away from there."

I remained silent for a while, and when I opened my eyes I saw Michael standing in front of me. For a very short moment after I opened my eyes, his face was full of a compassion such that I had never seen before, but then quickly his face changed and he again looked relaxed and smiling. He gave me his hand silently, helping me to stand. He didn't say anything, and we continued to walk through the ruins of Afrasiab.

Chapter 7

Soon we reached the edge of the valley and I saw a house on the hill. It was an ordinary Uzbek adobe building painted white and surrounded by thin poplar trees. A simple sign stating "Museum" was posted on its closed door. Michael chose a round white stone near a poplar tree and sat on it.

"This is the place for telling the stories," he said. "You started telling me your stories, and now it's my turn to tell you mine as I promised."

I looked around and didn't see any other stone to sit on. But then I noticed a small wooden bench, not far from the museum's door, and sat on it, so that Michael was about six feet away from me. The distance wasn't that comfortable for a conversation, but since I couldn't change it, I decided not to pay attention to the discomfort.

"The story you just told me is the next layer that covers your sadness. It belongs to the same space inside you from which your sad feeling comes. You went deeper and recovered that memory. It was very important to do and you did it well. It is not a child's story about losing her cat. You believe that you were guilty for not saving your cat. You believe that you could have done something differently and then the cat would have been saved. You probably know now in your mind that a five-year-old child could do little in that situation, but it is in your mind. In your feelings, you believe that you are guilty."

I was silently nodding my head, agreeing with his words.

"The fact that the trauma is irreversible makes it more painful," Michael continued. "You feel powerless because of the finality of it. It hurts so much because you feel guilty for not preventing the death and because you can't change the death after it happened. This is a real thread to something that lies at the core of your trauma, something you need to remember next."

I felt uneasy, but continued listening to him without interruption.

"Now let me tell you something else. It's not as final as your mind is afraid it is. The sense of finality comes from the limits your understanding faces when it reaches the concept of death. You don't have to be afraid of death here, though this place has seen a lot of it. This place is among very few where people have been working with death consciously, and they have gathered some experience. They knew that the substance of death and dreams is the same, that the difference is only in the degree of intensity. They specifically worked with dreams here because it brought them closer to controlling death."

"People can't control death. It is not something one can control," I said.

"Of course they can. Death is a subjective experience. When you are scared of death, you are not scared of your body being in pain. You are scared of how you may feel what is called death. This is a purely subjective experience, and subjective experience is something you *can* control. After you have been trained properly. The same is true with your dreams. You think you can't control them. But do you know how? Do you know the essence of dream substance? If you knew, you would learn quickly how to do it. People in this place were very knowledgeable in this. They knew how to work with dreams. They had knowledge."

Michael grew silent, gazing in front of him for a while, his eyes unfocused and wide open, as if observing scenes from the past unfolding in front of him. Then he closed his eyes. He lifted his head and turned it to the sun. His eyes were moving slightly under the eyelids, as if he were seeing some images, while his face seemed remote and relaxed. I thought he had forgotten about me. Then he opened his eyes, looking straight to the sun, and I realized with surprise that, since we met this morning, a few hours must already have passed.

"The only way to gain knowledge from this place is through exchange. It has to be personal. You can't obtain knowledge by just making the decision to do so. You have to exchange your story for it. And you have to learn the stories of this place and of the people who existed on this land. This will be a part of the exchange for you here.

"The stories of the people who underwent transformation here need to be retold now, so their experience can become animated again, complete their transformations, and accelerate the transformative experience for the people who will hear their stories. This land wants to tell these stories for the people in other lands so they can obtain knowledge from them. The psyches of ancient people need to come back to life to activate memory changes in the people living now.

"The traumas of people from the past continue to live in their modern-day descendants even though most of them don't have any awareness of it. Telling their stories will help to heal these ancient traumas and change something critically important in the lives of many modern people. So you will have to retell these stories later, after you hear them from me and you return to your home."

He looked at me and when he saw in my face that I would rather hold back from any commitments, he added, "It is more a matter of responsibility than of choice. I often work for this place even when I don't feel like it, as if this ruined city was pushing me. But I know that I am among only a few people who can tell the stories of this place, and I have to do it. It is more difficult for places to present their stories, because only people can create and tell stories, so places need us to keep and tell their histories."

That said, he continued after a short pause, "This place is very old. It has layers of history. They connect; they influence each other, and continue to have a life, keeping a connection with us through direct lines of power transmission. I am connected to the oldest face of this town, to the very beginning of what is now called Afrasiab. Do you know who he is, this Afrasiab?"

"I know it is a name of this old town. Is it a person's name, too?"

"It is a person's name. Afrasiab.

"There is an old legend about him. Some parts of it were lost, some were intentionally erased from people's memories, but the legend is still alive. I will tell it to you as I learned it. And even though you may find some parts of it strange and confusing, it has to be told this way. It says that Afrasiab was as fearless as a tiger. He was a ruler of this place at the time of the Golden Time, the time when the world didn't know division. He served his god with devotion and received power in return."

Michael remained silent for a while, as if thinking what he could and couldn't say.

"Who was his god at that time? That was a long time ago, right?"

"His god was a god of sun and of Alive Time, a ruler of the sky and a commander of thunder. By his god's will, sacred waters of life flowed from the top of the world mountain and gave birth to everything alive. His god was a woman, Great Mother Anakhita, and Afrasiab served her like a tiger. He was faithful and devoted because he knew her love. Women were equal with men then and power was distributed equally. Anakhita had both men and women priests who served her. Afrasiab was not one of them, but he built the temples of fire, serving Anakhita throughout his kingdom, and he protected these temples. They were called *sufa*, and you may still find the remains of some of them when you walk eastward through the ruins.

"In *sufa* they preserved the Golden Time, until it started to change from jealousy. Two brothers were the highest priests of Anakhita. One of them, Zaratashta, at some point started to think that he should have more power than his brother. He became the enemy of his brother and the enemy of the goddess who gives life. She learned of his desire when he prepared to steal her sacred treasure and she ran away with it. He ran after her. When he was about to grasp her, she tore the necklace she wore that contained the treasure and threw it to the bottom of a lake hidden at the base of the mountain. She filled the lake with the milk rain, and hid the treasure.

"So Zaratashta became powerless and angry, and he promised to get revenge.

"The goddess removed herself from this world because she knew that jealousy had already settled in it. She hid herself in the star Sirius which had been her home before. She continued to rule from there. Afrasiab, who learned this story, didn't sleep, didn't eat, but walked miles and miles until finally he found that secret lake. There was an island in the middle of the lake with the *Haoma* tree growing on it. The *Haoma* tree contained the juice which

Anakhita used to connect the Earth and the stars where she used to live before coming to the Earth.

"Afrasiab camped near the *Haoma* tree and learned about the lake. He learned that the treasure was hidden at its bottom, at the deepest roots of the tree. He learned from the white bird living on the tree how to gather seeds from the *Haoma* tree. He threw them into the circle of sacred fire in the *sufa* which he built on the island, just as the white bird taught him. He breathed in a smoke from the sacred fire and attained power.

"Taking off all his clothes, Afrasiab dived into the lake three times, and at the third dive, he reached the treasure at the bottom. It was the key to immortality. Goddess Anakhita saw this and was pleased with his courage. From her home on Sirius, she sent down to Earth forty beautiful men and women, forty ancient spirits to serve Afrasiab.

"After two thousand earthly years, Afrasiab decided to leave the Earth. He made a mysterious creation as Anakhita taught him: a temple-fortress made of a shiny metal shaped in a perfect spheroid form, hermetically closed. He hid himself in it. Inside were artificial stars, including a sun and moon. Their light illuminated a wondrous garden. Afrasiab had everything he wanted inside this temple. His two thousand years of earthly life almost over, Afrasiab was ready to raise his temple to the top of the highest mountain, where Anakhita visited a few times each year. To be closer to her in those times, he created seven shining columns which could have transported the temple to the mountain top.

"But on the very last day of his two thousand years, when he was walking through his garden, he saw a man, who was dark complexioned, his face hidden. He approached him carefully and the moment he looked at him, Afrasiab recognized it was his own shadow, walking on its own, as if it were another being.

"This happened because the jealousy of Zaratashta was carefully preserved throughout this time and Zaratashta was waiting for the end of the Golden Time on Earth for his revenge to come. His poison reached Afrasiab's temple and Afrasiab saw his own shadow through it. Yet all happened by the will of great goddess Anakhita. She knew that soon the Golden Time would be gone, replaced by rivalry, and that people would forget her knowledge. She chose for Afrasiab the fate of sacrifice, of becoming the Alive King of the Dead because he had a treasure of immortality, so he could help people in their transition from life to what is beyond death in the coming time when they would forget her love.

"The spheroid temple-ship of Afrasiab never went to the highest mountain. It disappeared from our world. It went to the world of ancestors where Afrasiab became the first human King of the Dead.

"Since that time, the temple-fortress of Afrasiab appears as a shining spheroid ship among the mountains and flies between the kingdom of ancestors and Anakhita's kingdom. He helps those who die to be saved from the second death."

Michael fell silent and kept looking into the sky and then said in a soft voice, before I had a chance to ask him what he meant by second death, "That was the beginning of the battle. We carry the consequences of it in our memories in the way we record experience. It affected both individual and collective memories. The memory became divided and many shadows were created. When Zaratashta promised to get revenge, he knew he wouldn't do it himself; he waited for it to be done differently. His memory of anger and fear streamed like a fluid through memories of generations of his descendants, looking for a place to settle. Finally, it found a boy who was always second in things. He knew it hurt not to be first. His older brother served Anakhita as a priest, while the boy was allowed to serve not the goddess but her son, Akhura Mazda. In his life, love was lacking. Serving her son didn't resolve the hurt of envy of his brother, so he became obsessed with becoming *the first*. He left his tradition, family, and house, and traveled to other lands to preach his own beliefs and to become the first of all priests. This boy's name was Zoroaster.

"He allowed Anakhita's temples to be destroyed so his brother's faith wouldn't be above his and so his brother wouldn't be the first. He would. To become different, Zoroaster had to change the tradition to its opposite. In the place of unity he put separation. Everything was separated into two: black and white; good and bad; first and last. That was the final end of the Golden Time.

"The boy became the first to install new rules. To keep them, he had to change the culture's memory. In his preaching, he blamed Afrasiab for all sins and made him an enemy in the eyes of his people. Zoroaster darkened his name, but only on the surface, since 'underground,' Afrasiab still remains the living king, and forty ancient spirits still support him at the will of goddess Anakhita.

"You don't know much about Zoroaster and his teaching, but your psyche is still organized by the rules of division that he established. Awareness was moved away from the center of being by dividing everything into black and white, with shadows created on both sides. There are different ways to overcome dividing and to avoid the shadows. This is one of the things that can help you."

Michael took a little fragment of ancient pottery from his pocket and gave it to me. I saw the similar fragments under our feet on the dusty trails as we walked through the hills of Afrasiab. The one that Michael gave me had a simple drawing of a swastika on its surface, and it looked exactly like the other pictures of swastikas I had seen on the walls of ancient monuments as I walked near them yesterday.

"This is a very powerful symbol that can resolve the dividing of our psyches," said Michael, while I continued looking at this small fragment which easily fit in my palm. "Its four arms connect the right and left sides of our brain, and by doing so, they connect past with present. They also connect action and perception in a way that is different from our usual experience, so a sense of unity is created in the center of the symbol. This experience doesn't fall into separate memory spaces, but serves as a gate to the Golden Time, to undivided time.

"The image of the swastika is very important for the work that has been done in our tradition of dream healing. Its sides connect past and present, action and perception in a special way, and its center connects directly with all the memory spaces. When you know how to activate this symbol and how to work with it, the center of this image serves as a gate that opens to the dream space. In that space, all the memories ever recorded are connected, and through that space they can be accessed and transformed. The center doesn't have any shadows. It connects with each experience in memory directly.

"The center of this figure is an entrance to the dream space, and when you know how to work with it, it will give you the experience of particular types of dreams: *lucid* dreams, in which action and perception are united in a way totally different from our usual experience. There is only one experience in daily life that unites action and perception, past and present in the same way as lucid dreams do. It is the experience of orgasm. Its unity can be also used for healing the memory demons but it is not our way of practice. We work with dreams and heal through dream space.

"Lucid dreams are the closest experience to death that one can achieve while physically alive. I belong to the tradition of healers who heal memory demons in order to heal humans from the ultimate trauma, the trauma of death. As I told you already, the only difference between death and dream substance is the intensity of your awareness. In death, what you call subjective experience becomes completely objectivized. Lucid dreams are the way to prepare for that through working with the more subtle dream substance and making healing changes before memory demons solidify and hurt you in death. Lucid dreams protect you from the hurt of memory demons, and in lucid dreams you can become strong enough to conquer them.

"In regular life, memory demons take power over us by using memory images that cause depression and anxiety. In lucid dreams, you can't be depressed nor can you be anxious. You would lose the experience immediately. Take this symbol with you; it will help you tonight."

I held the swastika image in my hand, but I hesitated to take it with me. Michael understood my doubts.

"It was used for thousands of years before the Nazis. It was used for healing and balance, never for harm or destruction, until then. The reason the Nazis used it reversed was that there were people among them whose identities represented memory demons. They were full manifestations of the spirits of trauma and they tried to disarm the strongest weapon that could have been used against them. That is why they reversed the swastika, to protect themselves from its healing power. They lost. They always do.

"It is just a matter of time in which complete healing occurs, but sooner or later the memory demons become healed. Yet they keep coming back, and they multiply through different people in history, continuing to hurt the collective memory. There is presently a lot of work that needs to be done to heal them. So take this symbol with you to the hotel and don't be afraid of it. Come here tomorrow around noon. But please don't think about what to say tomorrow.

"Let it stay ahead of you in a space where your thoughts can't reach it yet and can't change it. Let the process that started in you continue through your dreams tonight. The swastika will help. Think only of what you see around you and have a safe trip back. I'll see you here at noon. Bring a shawl to cover your head. It will be a hot day tomorrow."

Chapter 8

I walked back alone, through the soft hills of Afrasiab with the long chain of Shakh-i-Zendeh mosques stretched out on my right. I remember a feeling from that walk—not a thinking, not a reasoning, but a deep, complete feeling engulfing my body. I would describe it as a mixture of deep, archaic energies, coming from far away in time, and high cosmic forces, coming from spaces far away. At that time, I didn't assign any description to it. I just felt myself walking along the dusty road, knowing I would go back there tomorrow. I was not looking forward to it, but simply walking toward it as my inevitable future.

When I came back to Samarkand, it wasn't as late as I had expected. Time had a different quality and pulsated with a different rhythm here than in any other place I had visited.

The bazaar plaza was crowded at this late afternoon hour, with many people shopping after work. I found a small shop with a wooden sign that announced "Fabrics."

It was a little cool inside that shop, which was a tiny semi-darkened room. Piles of silk fabrics rested on a narrow counter, and many shawls of different sizes and colors were displayed on the wall.

A white silken shawl caught my eyes. Of a plain beauty, it looked to be not too expensive. I asked to look at it, and a teenage girl who was helping her father, talking to another customer, handed it to me. Its surface was soft as a baby's skin and its color, when brought closer to the light, was more of a cream color than pure white. I bought it right away, without thinking.

"It will be a hot day tomorrow," I remembered Michael saying. I noticed that everything he said carried more authority for me and it was becoming difficult for me to question why I should trust him at all. I just did, and I didn't want to think about why.

Michael didn't ease my burden. He probably increased it. But his presence had a special quality. I experienced him more as a dream figure than a common human being. His presence made my experience in Samarkand closer to a dream reality, and Michael was my connection with that dream space—the real Master of Dreams, as I would later learn.

I still felt a basic anxiety filling my body, especially when I entered my hotel room. It had been cleaned while I was gone, and my stuff had been packed into the corner as if I didn't belong here. It looked foreign, as if it belonged now to a different world—the modern world where people lived with their rules and regulations and thought they could predict the future. This was a world I knew I had left behind, though I could still witness it by watching TV, examining the inside of my bags, or using the telephone. It would be so easy to dial a number and get connected to any of these "modern" people. Except I didn't want to.

I was adjusting to the position of being an observer rather than a participant in that world. It was scary, but I felt that it was the only right thing for me to do. To let go of my modern world defenses and trust Michael. That felt right.

I checked for messages at the front desk as I returned to the hotel that evening. There were none, and when I checked it the next morning and a few days after, there were still none. It didn't upset me, for somehow I didn't care about messages anymore. What was happening with Michael made me forget Vladimir, and I stopped waiting for him.

Night came over the city quickly. I felt so tired from the day that the moment I lay in bed and put the swastika symbol under my pillow, sleep came over me and I found myself inside a dream. It was a weird dream: I am back in Russia. I walk through Moscow's Red Square, which is empty at this twilight hour. It's cold, and the snowy wind blows in my face. I turn around and see a black car approaching me. It stops on my left, waiting for me to get in. As soon as I sit in the front, it starts moving very slowly as if it is part of some ceremonial procession. I don't see the face of the driver, but sense his presence, and I sense something strange, something inexplicably strange about this presence. I feel that there are people sitting behind me in the back of the car, but I can't look at them either.

I watch the dark, ancient brick pavement of the square through which we slowly move.

I see a group of people coming into the right corner of the square. These are only children moving abreast, keeping their rows perfectly organized. Their leaders play drums, marking the rhythm for their passage; their faces are serious and concentrated. Scarlet silk scarves flutter around their open necks. The column marches directly toward our car. The children come closer and closer and I can see their separate faces. I don't recognize any face in particular, but all of them create the impression I have seen them long ago. They don't notice me and they don't see the car. We move toward each other slowly but unavoidably.

They are right in front of me now, just a few yards away, but the speed of our mutual approach does not change. I still can't turn my head toward the driver to ask what's going on. So I sit there, frozen, watching these adamant children moving closer.

My inability to change something gives rise to a terror inside. I am almost paralyzed with fear, for I see that something awful is about to happen. The massive black car is going to reach these children in a second, but they still don't see it. There is nothing to stop the tragic crushing of bodies which will take place. I try to scream, but can't. I try to close my eyes to avoid seeing the bloody scene, but don't have control over my eyelids anymore. With my eyes wide open, I have to watch the scene of horror unfolding before me. When the faces of the children in the front rows are in front of me, my terror reaches its climax.

The next moment, my breath bursts out of my throat in a scream. First, their hands holding the drums, then their school scarves, their figures, their faces freely penetrate the front of the car, passing through the seats, through my body. I am relieved from my fear, but shocked. The marching children are of a matter different from the car. They don't feel my touch; they can't hear my scream; they just keep going proudly as if nothing had happened at all. Passing through me and the car, they disappear somewhere behind me. I can turn around and see now.

I see the driver, a young man in a black wool coat with a round face and steady profile. His head is shaved and his light blue eyes are fixed magnetically on the road. I turn to the back seat. I know something abnormal is happening to me, and I know that the people sitting in the back seat have the answer to it. I see two small human figures sitting next to each other, their hands calmly placed on their knees. They look at me, understanding exactly what is going on in me. Horror embraces me again.

These figures are humans with bird heads, big feathered heads with extended beaks, and their black, birds' eyes examine me. The reality of their presence, which I feel strongly, tells me something horrible, irreparable has happened to me.

"Has something happened to me already?" I dare to ask them, knowing they can understand my words and my innermost feelings.

They don't have the mouths to talk, so they nod their heads, confirming that my suspicion is true. When I see their slowly moving bird heads, the realization reaches my awareness and comes out of me, almost against my will, in my next question. "Have I died already?"

Even before their heads move the same way again, I know the answer. A profound sadness and melancholy saturate me. The doors have been closed to the only existence I knew of my life. I don't have the keys to unlock it again. I lose the entrance there. I am left in a world in which people with bird heads rule, and I don't have any knowledge or protection or guidance to help me.

I woke up suddenly, sadness rooted in my body. This dream didn't make any sense, but its imagery was so deep and complete that I didn't need the anxiety anymore to hide from myself the reason for this sadness. It opened the space of my deepest trauma; it showed me the covered spaces of my memory which I was trying to avoid. And I knew that now I would have to deal with it, that there was no more escape from my guilt and sadness for me.

The children's scarves were still fluttering in my mind, and I automatically touched my neck, trying to untie the scarlet silk as if it were still around my neck and suffocating me. The dream released something in me, and I understood that now I would be able to tell Michael what had been troubling me.

I had time before noon the next day, and after having breakfast in the hotel I walked outside and stopped in a bookstore. Before the collapse of the Soviet Union, many books were written in Russian, then the official language in Uzbekistan, and I browsed through them. I was trying to find the description of the tradition Michael was teaching, but couldn't find any direct references. Books on Sufism were the closest, but their concepts were different. I couldn't find anything specific about the tradition of the dream healers. Before leaving the store, I opened a large volume called *Mythological Dictionary* and opened it to "ch." The page had a short description of the word *chiltan*.

It said, "*Chiltan* comes from the Persian for 'forty people.' In Central Asian traditions they are described as forty invisible powerful spirits who govern the world. *Chiltans* often are invisible to people, but they also can live as regular human beings among common people. Uzbek myth says that *chiltans* live on a remote island which no human can reach. They gather occasionally to discuss their business in secluded places, near burial grounds, near ancient sites. According to beliefs of some Uzbek groups, *chiltans* were the first shamans and the first shamans' guardians. Sometimes they appear as forty beautiful young men and women, dancing at night."

I couldn't connect this bit of information with the woman's words in the bazaar yesterday. I closed the book, dismissed this unrelated information, and went to Afrasiab to see Michael.

He was there before me. I saw him from a distance as he was jumping over the narrow crevices between some hills. His body looked so light it was almost weightless, and obviously these jumps were very easy for his fit body. When I came closer, he said, "Hi," then jumped quickly to the other side of the deep well that penetrated the ancient ground. The well was a little wider across than a usual stride, but it was so deep that I could see only its perfectly round walls going down into the earth, but not the bottom. Michael was standing on the other side of the well, and before I walked around it to come closer to him, he stopped me. "No. Don't walk here. Just jump."

I looked down into the well again. It was a dark tunnel without end, and its size was sufficient to let my body fly downwards to its bottom should I fall into it. "Thank you, but I don't feel like it," I said as calmly as I could, hoping that he would drop the subject.

"Why not?" He obviously didn't want to drop it.

"Because it doesn't make much sense, and I simply don't want to."

"Do you feel afraid?" He was looking at me intently.

"Maybe, maybe not. I don't even want to explore why I don't want to jump over this stupid well."

"Oh, you are even getting angry over it. Why is that, Olga? You are quite a nice person. Why would you resist this simple suggestion?"

"The way you ask it, Michael, it sounds like you know why I feel this way. Why do *you* think I don't want to do it?"

"It's simple. Because it would lead you away from the patterns of fixation. Fixation is a mechanism by which the psyche holds its separateness, and it is the mechanism that memory demons use to preserve themselves inside different memory compartments. When your energy flows, when your body is flexible, when you can jump over abysses easily, then your psyche functions differently and your memory lets go of all hidden and separated spaces easily—to become whole with the rest of your psyche. Plus, it's just fun to jump over wells."

This last phrase made Michael look like a boy who was having fun jumping wells, and I felt my initial anger disappear. I looked again down the well, but its depth made me uncomfortable.

"You know, Michael, I do feel afraid to jump over it," I said in a nice voice, hoping that, now that I had admitted it, he would drop the subject. He laughed with pleasure. Nothing about my internal process could stay hidden from his attention, I thought.

"You can use it as an exercise," he insisted. "The best skill you can teach yourself is to learn how to switch perspectives, to change the position of your subject. This is what you did yesterday with the rope on the ground. While you keep thinking about your action, your memory remains active and it pushes you from one point of fixation to another, and that complicates the purity of your movements. You look into this well and have countless associations going through your mind. If you try to jump in this state of mind, you may really fall into it, even though technically there is very little chance of it. But most likely you would, because your fear is so active that it would push you to fall. I don't want that to happen. What I want you to do is to try to position your attention so that it is unreachable by fearful memory, and then to jump with joy. Use as much space as you need to change your perspective. Look at yourself from far above. Experience your body from a distance. It may help you to experience your fears from a distance, as if they do not belong to you."

As he was talking, my perception shifted, and I experienced myself as a point flying high above my body, connected to it with a very strong cord. This cord was resilient and secure and it didn't take any effort for me to jump into the air and to let my body fly over the well. It was easy to do, and it was fun.

I looked at Michael after my feet landed softly on the other side of the well and said, "Thank you."

"You are welcome," he answered with a smile. We walked toward the museum in the same way we had the day before. He didn't ask me anything and I didn't feel it was time yet to tell him my story. He started talking and I listened attentively as we approached the museum.

"After Afrasiab was made the Alive King of the Dead by goddess Anakhita here, this place became a battlefield. The separation of trauma from awareness in human memory was initiated here, and because of this, the potential for healing is also the highest in this place. Throughout the centuries people have been attracted to Samarkand because here it was easier to make their final choice to either be healed and transformed, or to give themselves completely to the memory demons which become very active in this territory. This place has seen a lot of hurt since the time of Afrasiab. People hurt others when they feel scared. That is the law. The more one hurts, the more fears one feels inside.

"The main reason for feeling scared is giving up the power of yourself. People won't give it up by their free will, but they do it all the time when they have been hurt. When they don't want the hurt to be a part of their personal memory, they reject the traumatic experience altogether. They don't accept it as a completed part of themselves so a memory demon catches it and states, 'This is mine.' The memory demon gets the energy; the self loses it.

"The gap in one's personal story has been created and it is always experienced thereafter as fear. When we feel fear, we feel this gap between what we know as our accepted memory and what belongs to some dark corner inside us. The fear returns again and again to hurt us. And through us it hurts others, and through this it feeds its secret memory.

"There was another boy whose fate was connected to this city. I will tell you his story now because it needs to be told. You will take it with you and you will tell it to other people, and through that process the healing will be expanded. His name will carry the healing out to people who know his name. When they hear this story from you, they will participate in healing his past and in healing their own present. There are many stories about him in people's memory, but I will tell you my version from a different perspective, from a perspective of hurt, fear, and transformation.

"He had different names here in Samarkand and in his homeland. His people remember him as 'the Great.' Our people remember him as 'the Horrible.' Alexander the Great. Iscander the Horrible. Boys grow to become world leaders when their personal gaps and fears connect deeply with those of the collective. The abused child who is born into the nation that was abused can use the power of his trauma to change the history of his nation. But in the end, if he doesn't achieve healing, he always turns from being a victim to a brutal traumatizer, and he creates more fear and suffering than he initially tried to resolve. That transformation from victim to traumatizer happened to Alexander here in Samarkand when he finally reached this city.

"He had a turning point in his life, a point of choice where he could have stopped and healed himself from the scars of his childhood. He could have helped his father and grandfather to be finally free from the effects of their early, brutal deaths and to find peace. But he was filled with memory demons when he reached Samarkand, or Maracanda, as the Greeks called it.

"The memory demons overfilled him since Egypt, where he had accepted the belief that he was a Pharaoh, not a human being but a divine being, one who was born from God and didn't need his earthly father. It was in Egypt that he refused his father and rejected all his memories of him. It was then he lost a chance to be healed from his childhood traumas and to become a great leader. After that turning point, it was not Alexander, not his self, but the memory demons that began to rule, and Alexander the Great turned into Iscander the Horrible.

"He destroyed Samarkand, which would have surrendered to him peacefully to preserve itself. His people killed, burned, and raped on these streets. He trembled with fear coming from the depths of his memory. He gave up his power of self and replaced it with a perpetual fear that wouldn't let him go. The fear from his past followed him like a shadow.

"He ran to the priests, to the fortune tellers, but the fear showed its face in every sacrifice they made for him, in every prediction they made for his future. Remember, when people feel fear, they hurt others. Alexander started to hurt like crazy.

"When his army crossed the River Oxus and came to our land, a huge crowd came out of the city to greet him. They were dirty, wild, ragged men, women and children, screaming and gesticulating with green branches. Descendants of Hellenic slaves brought by Xerxes to work on the Eastern borders of his empire, they spoke an old form of Greek. They greeted him wildly, but he stood there frowning, then suddenly he ordered his soldiers to kill them all. No one had time to run away, and all died. Aristotle heard about his agony and sent his pupil, Kallisten, here to help Alexander. But Alexander locked the philosopher in a cage and hung him as a plotter against his power. Everybody now looked suspicious to him; everybody seemed to be against him and deserved to die. His best friends, his brave warriors—all fell one after another at the hands of his fear.

"His last chance was given to him here by Roxana. He killed her father but she still married him. She knew the way of Anakhita and she gave herself to Alexander to stop the hurt. She calmed him down. He remembered himself with her; he felt moments of happiness when she dissolved his fears the way Anakhita taught her. She was preparing him for death. Some people say that our sorcerers joined with Babylonian magicians through the Mirror of the World which they had been holding between each other and destroyed Alexander, so when he left here to go to India he was destined to die. I say his own memory demons killed him, and no sorcery generated them for him. They were his own creations and they created his fears.

"It is true that when a person is filled with fears, he becomes vulnerable to any type of psychic influence because he has lost a connection with himself, the connection being the ultimate protection. But Roxana was protecting him and taught him secret knowledge about death and what is beyond so he could finally free himself from his memory demons. He was ready to die when his fears were blowing up his body, when they clouded his mind and made him crawl in pain. He was vomiting his fears, freeing himself from their chains. He let them go along with his agonized body, the way Roxana showed him, through love. He finally reached the peace he was striving for throughout his life at the very end of it. Roxana died soon after him, along with their son."

As Michael finished his story, I felt sad again. He had talked about death and it hurt me with its irreversibility. I remembered his talk yesterday about controlling death, but I couldn't accept his words completely. There was a gap in my perception between my desire to believe that what he was saying was true and my deep sadness caused by the finality of death.

"Tell me, Michael. Why do you think people can control death?"

"I don't think it. I know it." He looked at me with heightened interest. "Why did you ask that? Did you find the core of your trauma?" Though he asked in a nice way, I didn't know how to tell him, even though I knew exactly what I was supposed to say. "Tell me about the dream you had last night," he asked me.

I knew Michael was trying to help me start talking. I sat on the bench across from the museum entrance and told him my dream without looking at him. I told him about a black antique car, rows of children, and people with bird heads. I didn't give him any interpretations but just described the images.

Michael listened attentively. When I finished, he got up from the stone he was sitting on and took a few steps back and forth in front of the bench. Then he stopped in front of me, leaned in towards me, looked in my eyes, and said, "When you see yourself in a dream as somebody who died while you are still alive, then you are seeing somebody who died, but continues to live *within* you, and who continues to be a part of your memory. This comes as a next level of your memory, uncovered through the dream by your story about the death of your cat yesterday.

"You moved inside your memory following the map I suggested for you, and using memory spaces as keys, you reached this core. Because of the way you moved through your memory to reach this point, I can now tell you what I think is at the core of your trauma and help you talk about it. I can tell you that someone you cared about died, mostly likely in a violent death. You feel guilty that you didn't do anything to prevent this death. You feel guilty that it happened this way, and you feel profoundly sad because of the finality and irreversibility of what happened to that person."

I nodded my head, silently agreeing with his words.

"You also think that because you failed to help that person, you can't help anyone, and therefore you can't heal people anymore. This is where the memory demon is trying to take over your power and to make you defenseless, so you will get stuck in these feelings and beliefs, and indeed, never help anybody else. Tell me, Olga, who is that person? What was his name?"

"Her name." I felt that I was finally able to tell Michael the story.

Chapter 9

I thought I felt ready. But later I understood fully how difficult, and often even impossible, it is to talk or even think about what had once caused pain, because every return to that memory makes the pain as actual and unbearable as it was months or even years ago. Michael knew that, of course. And I think in me, in my internal movements, he saw exactly (as a surgeon sees a disease and the ways to eradicate it inside the open body on which he operates) how to control the process of my healing so I would have enough strength to complete it.

Instead of prompting me to go on with my story, he said unexpectedly, "You know what—why don't you take a little break before telling your story and listen to me? I will tell you what happened in Samarkand, centuries after Alexander. I will tell you this story not to interrupt you, but to help you to move farther into the space of healing you need. It will also help you use the healing energy of the intense process that you are going through now and bring it to the people of the past and to their present descendants to help them be healed. Don't look at me like that. You know I know that death is not final. You should know by now that I have a very different understanding of time, and of how past, present, and future are connected—that I know it is never too late for healing to occur.

"Centuries after Alexander, another boy was born. He was light, he was born from light, as his parents believed, from a small ball of light brought to Earth by the will of the Great Shaman. His hair was light; his eyes were light green; his skin was pale, but his inner spirit was fiery. Shamans protected him as a special child, for he was born in a noble family and had all the signs of a remarkable fate awaiting him.

"But one day their protection failed. The boy's father was killed first. The boy's family was left unprotected. His mother was a very strong woman but not strong enough to protect herself from the rage of wandering nomads. One day the enemy's horses smashed the remains of the boy's house and burned it to the ground. And he, a funny pale boy, so different from the others, was made a slave. His enemies put wooden stocks over his legs so he couldn't run, and he couldn't walk either. He lived like a dog, and grew up like a dog, chained outside, eating rotten food, freezing on winter nights, wishing for death. But it spared him. He survived.

"When he finally escaped, his character was changed. He knew his name now would be his war cry, and it would cause terror and death to anyone who would dare to disobey him. He was destined to save his people and to return to them the dignity they deserved. When his name was pronounced, it echoed like thunder throughout all Asia. People heard his name and came to serve him. 'People of Long Will,' they called themselves, and the boy's name controlled and guided their will. His name as we remember it until now—Genghis Khan.

"We heard his name too when he came to our land, ages after Alexander. He was a great warrior and didn't know fear. He had an old shaman on his side who guided him through his visions. But the law is the law. If your memory gaps are not healed, if you reject your past, then you let the spirits of trauma in. Sooner or later, no matter how great you are, they come to torture you and to torture others through your actions.

"Genghis Khan's shaman was wise. He knew the law. He saw the threat of this transformation coming. He warned the boy, who was now the greatest leader alive, the ruler of the world at the top of his power. But the shaman knew the boy was still inside, scared, unprotected. It was a dangerous situation and his warning failed. Fear was in Genghis Khan's heart already when the old man talked to him. Fear was in control, making decisions. The decision was made to get rid of anything that stood in the way of fear. So Genghis Khan killed his teacher.

"When he came to Samarkand, his people destroyed the city. They killed so many people that very few were left. But he believed in magic, and he talked to the priests of these places and let them live. Because he had a feeling that this place could show him such magic as he hadn't known before. The priests of the Zoroastrian way were saved; they probably showed him some magic; but they couldn't save him from the spirits of trauma that were torturing him. Still he was given another chance, as Alexander had been.

"He saw a woman, one of a few who survived. She was a young girl, sitting on the ground in shock. Her family was killed; her house was burned. Her golden city didn't exist anymore. But death wasn't taking her, and she was lost, not knowing her fate.

"Her face was unusual: her complexion was light and her features were beautiful. Her eyes were light green and her skin was pale. She sat on the ground in silence. He saw her face and saw she looked much like his mother before they tortured her. The boy inside him cried; he heard the screams of his father. The sounds of clanging metal filled his ears. Images of flames darkened his vision, and he remembered how the fire had scorched his lips. That boy was still alive and he wouldn't stop crying tears he thought were gone long ago and didn't belong to him anymore. But they were back, tearing apart his lungs, boiling his blood, and he felt scared.

"The voice inside his head, the one that had calmed him down before, that had whispered 'Kill the shaman' before he killed him, talked to him again and made him believe that the boy had died. 'Just destroy everything that is in your way and this memory won't come back to you. I will take care of it.'

"Genghis Khan grasped the woman's long hair and threw her body to the ground. She was flexible like a doll. She didn't resist anything. Her eyes were open, looking at the sky. She felt better now because she knew her fate. The sky was clear and there were no clouds, and the sun was right above them. He tore apart her silk dress; her breasts were warm and her body smelled like milk. The boy's voice came through his head and hurt his heart, and the whole world became filled with his cry.

"Black anger came upon Genghis Khan from the depth of his soul and turned him into an animal without memory who was raping her, tearing her apart, filling her with his rage so she would stop existing. She saw the sun and the sky high above her tortured body. The love in her didn't find its way to him, didn't resolve his fears.

"The Great Mother Anakhita took the girl away after his fears turned love into the opposite and Genghis Khan lost his chance to be saved. After she died, he pulled a white silk shawl off her head and covered her tortured body with it, as if the sun's rays could harm her. He walked away very slowly because his excruciating headache was worse with every step. He had to stop many times before it went away and he could walk normally again. He probably walked by the very road we walked this morning. The ruins of Afrasiab are where the city used to be before Genghis Khan leveled it. Samarkand arose from here. But that is another story."

"Why is it still called Afrasiab if it was Samarkand?"

"Because Afrasiab still lives in this city," said Michael. "I even think that he would be interested to hear your story." As before, it was difficult to say how much seriousness or irony was in his words. But this phrase sounded suddenly so light and easy after the story he had just told, that I felt now I could talk lightly and easily about anything, even about heavy, unpleasant things.

"My friend's name was Lara. She died by a violent death, and you are right in saying that I didn't do anything to prevent her death, and I think because of that I can't help anybody else."

"Olga, wait a second," Michael interrupted me. "Language is too powerful a tool to be ignored. I didn't say that you didn't do anything to prevent her death, I said that you *think* you didn't. It makes a huge difference. When you talk, think how you talk.

"Why do you think you didn't help her?"

"I think it was because the very last time I saw Lara, she asked me for help and I refused. That day when I last saw her, she—she was always so beautiful and radiant—but she was already exhausted by her depression to a great extent. I hadn't seen her for a while, and I was shocked to see how much she had changed. I had known her for many years—we went to school together for ten years, beginning at first grade—but I had never before seen her so drained and despondent. We met accidentally on the street. After a few ordinary remarks, she said straightforwardly that she would like to work with me. She always had been a very modest and delicate person, and if she ever asked anything for herself, it was only in a case of extreme need. Indeed, she was in much need of help. I guess she already realized that her own strength was not enough to overcome her depression, and she asked me to help.

"She was an important person in my life. I felt very close to her, even though we hadn't seen each other often lately. I appreciated her greatly and I thought I would always do anything for her if she needed it. But at that time, I felt overburdened with my own problems. I was going to work abroad and I told her politely and gently that I was leaving soon, but when I came back I would be happy to help her in whatever way I could. But deep inside I felt I was lying; on some level I knew that she didn't have enough resources to fight her depression and that this was the last time I would see her."

"You think that the cause of her depression was rape? And that it was your fault that you didn't ask her about it directly?"

Michael's question affected me as though I had been physically hit. This question was something that I didn't admit even to myself, yet it all seemed obvious to him, as if he knew in detail all the hidden facts of this story. His question was right, and it was the main question that I had kept asking myself since my last meeting with Lara.

I met her when her depression had taken her over, and it was obvious that what she was going through would soon destroy her if she didn't get help. Still, I didn't ask her about her depression or about the thing that had caused it, even though I had heard rumors about her being raped by a stranger one night. Michael wasn't guessing. He knew exactly what he was asking about. I didn't know how to answer him because I didn't know the answer.

Telling this story to him was difficult since it remained a part of my internal reality, and through many sleepless nights, its facts, circumstances, my assumptions about it, and things that I heard from other people about it were assimilated into one intense, painful feeling I was trying to avoid. I trusted Michael more than anybody else now. But I also knew that it would take more effort for me to tell him the rest of the story, maybe more than I felt able to make. I remained silent, not knowing how to answer his question.

"So why didn't you ask her about the rape?" Michael repeated. I didn't turn to him, but kept standing still, looking up at the sky.

I felt my legs go numb. Maybe it was from the long walk through the hills to the ruins. I quietly moved myself down, closer to the ground, which was wet and cool, just to feel its support and to not think about his question.

"You know, Michael, I think I need to go back to the hotel. I appreciate your listening. But I feel strangely tired, almost sick now. You probably are tired from listening to me, too. I think I should go."

"I think you should stay. And now I am not going to spare you with my stories. You have to finish yours, whatever it takes, and you have to do it honestly.

"The gap in the psyche I told you about before is a seat for a memory demon to anchor in to and grow. It is a parasite which tries endlessly to deceive you into believing it is an innermost part of you while it sucks your energy and makes you feed it with more fears. The gap is created any time something traumatic happens and the personality is not strong enough to accept it as a part of itself. The psyche takes it in as something foreign to itself. Then, when many of those experiences have accumulated, they become a nourishing substrate for another subject. Because it is brought up by trauma, one can call it the spirit of trauma. Everyone has it.

"More or less, we all carry these detached memories which become taken over by memory demons. They are inherited as the fears and traumas of our parents and ancestors. The spirits of traumas create yet more traumatic circumstances, again and again. They help people make excuses to avoid seeing them in the full light of day. They make people suddenly tired, uninterested, wanting to change the subject before the trauma's nature is uncovered. Like your wanting to return to the hotel now."

"So you are saying that my choices are controlled by the spirits of trauma, and they are guiding me to avoid seeing this?"

"I think you are experienced enough to recognize that. Remember your patients, those who will do everything to elude real healing. You are not much different from them now. And one more thing, I told you about jealousy and how dangerous it can be. Memory demons are full of jealousy. They fight for your attention and are in rivalry with any gift a person has. They will try to steal the gift and destroy it, so the person's attention will be occupied only by the fears the spirits create. In your case, this trauma is trying to steal your gift of healing to make you refuse to heal others who need it. That is the goal of your spirit of trauma, and you would serve it if you left now."

Michael stood against the setting sun, silhouetted by the pink sky and hills of Afrasiab. I thought how he was so handsome and fine, yet I didn't feel any attraction to him as to a man. His face was hidden in shadow, but I felt his soft smile through a slight change of his posture. Then I heard him laughing, a laugh so contagious I couldn't help but smile.

"Everything partial is more likely to increase the gap and feed the memory demons. Since you are thinking about sex, I can tell you that partial sex, sex without connection and understanding, does it more than anything else." I realized with tension that he sensed my thoughts somehow and was answering them.

"That's why many people feel traumatized after making love. They look for love to fill in their painful gaps, but get stuck with partial sex, which, even when rewarding physically, ultimately hurts them more. You don't feel any attraction to me because I practice a different way of experiencing love. But this is not what you want to talk about. Black and white at work again, Olga. You start thinking about making love to hide from what is opposite to it. It is rape, and this is what you want to talk about. Save us time, Olga."

"Okay. It never had been confirmed about Lara. There were rumors that she had been raped, but no one knew for sure. She just got lost for a few hours one night in late autumn, coming home from the late shift. She came home with some bruises and torn clothes. She didn't say anything bad had happened, and she never made a big deal out of it. There were just rumors. No one really believed them, not her husband or her father."

"Why you are so afraid to accept the prospect that she was raped?"

"Because I don't want to think that she had to suffer it."

"Why don't you want to think it?"

"Because I didn't want her to suffer."

"Didn't you tell me just now, inside your story, that you saw her suffering greatly and that you felt guilty for not helping her when she asked for it?"

"Yes."

"So you remember her suffering but you resist accepting that she had been raped that night? You are a professional, and a good one, I may say. Don't lie to me that you can't recognize the trauma of rape. I bet you can recognize it in the first few moments of your conversation with a patient. And you did. I bet you did recognize it in Lara, but refused to accept it, giving it to a part of your memory you don't think is yours. Lara was too good to be raped. Rape doesn't happen to good women. This is your first gap, as much as it was hers. Face it now.

"I can almost visualize her image as you try to hold it in your memory: an ideal, delicate woman, beautiful, untouched by dirt. She lives inside of you; you have her image in your memory nurtured by years of growing up together. She is projected like an icon for you, one who is always pure, always strong, and to whom you can turn in moments of confusion. You feel great relief that an ideal exists and can help you to make sense out of reality when-ever you need it. You provide therapy for yourself by hold-ing to this ideal. You won't let it go, even at the expense of letting the real person suffer. You close your eyes and ears in order not to hear about the ugly rape; you erase it from her story. This is hypocrisy, Olga, a huge gap you need to heal. Lara was a live person and her suffering is not symbolic but real. You need to help her."

Warm tears dripped down my cheeks. I couldn't say what I wanted to say and kept nodding my head. I didn't have a handkerchief to wipe my tears away, so they kept rolling down, reaching my lips, making me feel finally free from something heavy and ill. I didn't feel hurt by Michael's unexpected harshness. I felt that his severity was addressed directly to something in myself that wasn't me, something that I wanted to be free of. He was helping me to get rid of that falsehood with his harsh but true words.

His harshness was gone when I looked at him, and I saw that his face was full of compassion again. His eyes were focused on me with attention and understanding.

"Do you remember how we talked about the metaphor of physical movements and moving through your mem-ory?" he said.

I nodded.

"The concept of simple movement and movement complicated by the weight of mental constructs is true for moving through memory spaces as well. To walk through the spaces of your memory freely, you need to have as sim-ple a movement as you can. You need to be free from fears, anger, and frustration to reach the point in memory that needs to be transformed. Right now you still have much frustration in the way of moving through your story. Tell me what really disturbs you before you continue talking about Lara."

The sincerity of his intention to help me was so strong that it made me realize right away what he meant by asking his question.

"I don't want to think about those people," I said. Michael didn't ask me whom I meant, but waited for me to continue.

"I can't remain calm knowing that those people are still at large. I can't accept that she is gone and somebody who caused her death is still here. I can't accept it."

"You talk about people who rape, right? In the case of those people, their memories were caused by the hurts which they themselves experienced in the past at the hands of someone else. These memories can remain unconsciously active for a long time and then at some moment they become strong enough to take over identity. They become full manifestations of memory demons and then they start hurting other people. Such people stop being people and become representations of trauma. That's why many of them use drugs. They need drugs to fill in the gaps in their identity, to reconstruct a sense of self.

"The same is true for many other people who abuse drugs. They try to fill in the gaps in their memory in order to return the sense of identity disturbed by the hurt. But they can't achieve it with drugs, so they feel afraid. When they feel afraid, they may begin to hurt others.

"I told you about the Nazis. The same happened in other totalitarian societies. There were people among them whose identity became equal to their memory demons. The same is true for many serial killers and rapists. If not at all times, at the moment of committing the crime, their behavior is totally guided by memory demons. They *are* memory demons at those moments, and those memory demons feed themselves through hurting others.

"I understand how you feel. I understand your frustration. There are ways to transform those memory demons. Society has its own means to protect itself from such people. Magic has developed other ways, but magic can't coexist with anger and frustration because they lead you away from it. To fight the memory demons magically, you have to clear your internal spaces first, so that your memory wouldn't be vulnerable to their attacks. It is an extremely difficult task.

"Working with dreams can assist greatly in this task. Lucid dreams help clear internal spaces very quickly, because movement is an essential part of them. I gave you a swastika to work with because its shape accelerates the movement through memory spaces and facilitates lucid dreaming. You become more prepared for a magical fight. The memory space is populated by images. The memory demons can be seen as images too, but they have much more conscious energy in them than usual memories. And exactly because of that, when they are seen and transformed, they don't disappear, but change the quality of their energy and start serving you after you conquer them. This is how shamans obtain the most powerful spirit helpers. Many believe that shamans get their helpers through transmission from older shamans. This is true.

"But somewhere along the line, those spirit helpers were memory demons, who were transformed and subjugated by a shaman who turned them into obedient servants. It is a matter of the transformation of psychic energy. Lucid dreams and shamanic journeys are the best states for that. Now, tell me, how did Lara die?"

Chapter 10

"When I think about it, I don't have a coherent memory of her death. I remember only some pictures, scenes which I imagined from what others told me about her death. They are isolated scenes, and often come to me like stills from a movie, having a life of their own in my mind. I can't put them all together in one continuous story and tell it to you exactly, step by step."

"This is the traumatic gap, right here," said Michael. "You can't connect those pictures in your memory with previous experiences, and they stay isolated, having, as you said, 'a life of their own.' They have power over your attention, and can continue traumatizing you. Tell me what scenes you remember."

"I know that after that autumn night, Lara became a different person. It was as if the source of light was turned off inside her and the depression was filling her up. Her family didn't know what to do with her depression since she refused to discuss it with anybody.

"One day after I left to go abroad, far away in a Siberian apartment in the early morning, Lara's husband was helping her put on her long, ankle-length mink coat, as if she was a doll who couldn't move by herself. He helped her walk out into the dark hallway and go a few steps down the street, where his car was warming up for their long journey.

"She was being taken to see a *babushka*, an old renowned healer and fortuneteller in a village not far from the city. Lara didn't feel good. She refused to have breakfast, as she always had in the last months; she wasn't talking, and she was very weak. Her huge black eyes were fixed on the slippery winter road, and she didn't look around. She was focused inside herself, but paradoxically, her inner concentration made her eyes shine with intensity. When they stepped out of the car and reached the healer's house, she freed her hand from her husband's and walked alone.

"The house was a typical village home, which didn't differ much from many other houses around. *Babushka* was waiting for them and met them at the doorway. 'Come on in, my beauty. Come on in,' she said. Lara silently took off her coat, shaking it a few times to get rid of the snow that had covered the fur on the short walk from the car to the house. The husband was left in the waiting room, and the two women walked inside.

"The room had a large dinner table in the middle, icons in the main corner, and a smell of intense herb mixtures. Lara was told to sit at the table, and *Babushka* began her work. She looked at Lara's hands, then she threw out the pack of cards on the table. She asked Lara to shuffle them, and then, after having looked at them for a while, got up and left the room.

"She didn't really need any additional magic tools to foretell Lara's future; she didn't even need her cards. An eighty-year-old woman, having devoted her entire life to talking to people about their futures and to healing them from all possible pains, *Babushka* knew what pain she was dealing with. She needed a second out of the room to be free from the intense, direct gaze of the dark eyes of this beautiful woman, full of such suffering. She had taught herself lessons of an old witch doctor, her grandmother, through years of practice. She still remembered seventy years later how to make her body a perfect mirror and how to read correctly what was being reflected on its surface. That girl was a rare case. She was too perfect for the demons to let her go easily. To be freed, she needed to be fought for.

"The old woman shook her head as if throwing unnecessary weight off her shoulders and returned to the room with a clear glass filled with water. She placed the glass on the table on her right, and, looking at the cards, started mixing them slowly, bending her head over the glass from time to time, whispering something onto the water's surface as if she were talking to a person hidden in there.

"Lara sat quietly, looking at her with awakening interest.

"'Listen to me, girl,' said *Babushka*. 'You have let in a power that is many times larger than you. You feel now that you can handle it because you think that this is inside you and is part of you and that it makes you stronger and helps you forget the hurt you went through. But one day, it can take over, and you won't have the strength to resist it. My advice to you, beauty: don't cross the boundary. Stay away from it. Fight it. Run away. You can be saved. It's easier to do now than if you keep giving up pieces of yourself following its call. I can help you. Come to see me next week. We'll begin work and you'll be well.'

"Lara left the house confused but comforted. She felt this old woman understood what was happening to her and had some secret means to change her life back to where it used to be. When they were driving back, Lara was even talking to her husband, even if it was insignificant conversation; but it indicated this day *could* have been the turning point for her to heal.

"I am learning from you, Michael, about the memory demons, and the more I learn about them, the more I understand what Lara was going through. I now accept the spirits of trauma as a reality. I saw it in Lara. I now know that it is a real dimension, even though it belongs more to a psychological than a physical domain. And I believe that, exactly because of their intangibility, these demons can obtain power over our wills and take us over.

"Lara waited for her next meeting with *Babushka*, because, as we say in Russia, 'hope dies last.' Lara still hoped to break through the veil separating her from outside reality, and she believed the old woman had the power to help her. The second time she was going to visit *Babushka*, she went to the car quickly in anticipation of that visit. But when the car made one wrong turn after another and finally stopped in front of a high iron gate with a sign 'Psychiatric Hospital #3' on it, and a dismal security guard opened the gates, nodding to her husband silently as if he knew about their coming, she didn't ask why her husband changed his mind and she didn't resist. She just remained silent and followed them in.

"Anyone who has been in a hospital knows the basic anxiety that being there inevitably creates. You are a novice, and you probably are there not by your wish, but by the evil will of your disease. It's frightening. I think Lara was frightened. I am sure she thought that by entering this psychiatric ward she was confirming her mental abnormality, accepting that something was wrong with her mind. This is the most fearful of acceptances. Even though this ward was a new addition to the clinic, and was one of the first private wards in the city organized for patients with minor psychiatric problems, it was still inside the hospital's iron fence, still carried the stigma for its patients of being the crazy house.

"'A new one, eh?' said a young girl, her new roommate, when Lara walked into the room assigned to her.

"The girl jumped off her unmade bed, checked her short red hair, and leaned toward Lara, who was sitting stiffly on her new bed.

"'Varvara,' said the girl, introducing herself and extending her arm for a handshake. Her thin arm, palm to elbow, was covered with long, deep scars which ran through her skin like rows of purple wires. She knew well what impression her bare arms could create, and she read right away through Lara's face that she had never known about cutting and was too gentle to ask where the scars came from.

"So Varvara decided to wait, not to push, not to scare, just to take Lara over gradually but firmly. She would teach her gently but persistently, and by all means not give her to the stupid shrinks with all their ambitions and insecurities, who would come tomorrow, hungry to include this new one in their power games.

"Varvara knew better. When night came, she was ready. She heard familiar voices laughing from the nursing station and knew that the night shift would be busy now for a while, enjoying themselves. They wouldn't bother with a room check. She felt anxiety and anticipation pushing up her blood, making her veins swell, and she needed to pause for a moment to catch her breath.

"Lara was sleeping, motionless like a doll. It may be hard to wake her up quietly without a fuss, Varvara thought. She leaned down and took carefully from under her mattress a new steel razor she had exchanged for cigarettes during today's walk. The room was lit with artificial blue light and she saw very well where to sit on Lara's bed so Lara would see her better when she woke up.

"But Lara woke up before Varvara had planned to wake her. She opened her eyes and saw this red-haired girl with a bluish, exhausted face and nervously shining eyes sitting on her bed like a creature who had jumped into the room straight from her own recurring nightmare.

"Lara wasn't going to talk anyway, but the girl held her finger to her lips, motioning her to remain silent. Lara sat on her bed, back to the wall, and looked at the girl, waiting.

"In the dark, Lara's eyes were black and huge, and she was so solid in her silence and indifference that it made Varvara wonder if she had estimated her correctly. Looking at Lara made Varvara more nervous, more anxious, so she squeezed the cold metal of the razor in her hands tighter, reminding herself who was in control.

"The feeling of power mixed with a tension of now almost unbearable anxiety as anticipation overflowed in her. Varvara's gestures became slow as if she was under water; her vision was moving back and forth between darkness and flashes of pictures from the blue room with this strange woman in its corner. Varvara felt it was difficult to control her breathing now, and she was squeezing the razor tighter and tighter, gaining and losing control over her acts, her choices, her disobedient body, which she would master soon any way she wanted to. She knew the steel edge was touching her skin now, ready to penetrate it.

"Varvara cut too deep this time. The blood rushed down her arm in a stream, instead of in drops, and it brought a relief many times more intense than usual. She kept looking at her blood, as if it was the most beautiful sight she had ever seen. At that moment, it was a stream of power, magical, and it was taking away whatever wasn't hers and whatever was dangerous.

"She lifted her eyes to look at Lara. She wished so much to see in front of her her former roommate who would share with her the joy and who would understand how elated Varvara felt. But that roommate had transferred to another room a few days ago, and this new girl was far away from Varvara's true feeling, even when she asked her softly, 'Are you hurting?'

"But it wasn't the question. Sensitive to pain, Lara knew that it didn't hurt. But she didn't want to know why Varvara had done it and she didn't ask her anything.

"Varvara would feel irritated at her indifference, but at some other time, not now. The experience was too good to cloud it with anger now.

"'You don't understand,' she said in a whisper, returning to her bed and trying to put some of her blood into a small empty bottle in her robe pocket.

"'What hurts is different. You know it, I guess. First it hurts when it happens. When your body is being used and you have no power to stop it. No power whatsoever, and the more you try to resist, the more enjoyable your body becomes for them. *That* hurts a lot.'

"Varvara kept talking in a whisper, letting her blood in the bottle, drop by drop.

"'Then it hurts different. It hurts from inside, from the memory that burns, but you are too weak to deal with it. You try to look around and call for help, but before you even say anything to anyone, they betray you, all of them— your family, men, friends. They know your secret and they don't want to deal with it. They shut your memory away, tighter than even you can do, and they keep it shut so until you finally betray yourself. When that moment arrives, you accept that such things as rape happen only to bad people, only to bad women, for a good one would be saved, and if you were not saved you must be the doomed one. And other bullshit like this. That hurts the most.'

"'Cutting is power. It is all reversed. You take your power back through the hurt, because you are a chosen one and you learn how to achieve it. People have been doing it for centuries, people who were the chosen ones. It's in religions, you know, because it is mystical. Like Rasputin. Do you know what they did in their *khlysty* sect before he got power over all of Russia? They hurt themselves. Hurt themselves badly, let their blood out to obtain the force. But you have to experience it to understand.'

"She closed the bottle tightly, wiped her arm carefully to hide the traces of her cutting, and looked at Lara, who was still sitting motionless in bed.

"After their eyes met, Lara turned away and lay down on her bed. Before closing her eyes, she looked again to Varvara's side and said in a soft voice, 'I am sorry. I can't help you, Varvara. I can't help myself.'

"Then she remained silent for the rest of the night. They left her alone after that. Varvara and a couple of others decided in their day walk that she was too weird and not worthy to be included into their sacred rites. Lara was left alone.

"Soon she was discharged home with 'partial improvement.' And a few weeks later, on a spring Sunday, she took a bottle of acid and drank it all. After an hour of unthinkable pain, she died, and the ambulance crew was helpless to do anything to save her. I was told about it nine days after her death, at the airport after coming home from abroad. She didn't need my help anymore. It was too late."

Chapter II

When I was silent, Michael said, "I want you to know that there is a tremendous power in storytelling, Olga. Sometimes people can get healed from deepest hurt just through telling the story about it. You just did it and it will help you to move forward. Take a break now and listen to me.

"Our tradition cherishes the power of storytelling because it works with healing. We also believe that our dreams are the best storytellers, and through the stories of our dreams the deepest healing can occur. The nature of my work in our tradition of healing is to guard the gate to the dream space and, when necessary, to open those memories that require transformation. It is also to make sure that the memory demons that were healed and sent away through the dream healing never come back and stay isolated from human memory.

"It was necessary for you to hear the stories of the people from the past. I told you about the initial hurt that was born from the jealousy of Zaratashta in this land. I told you about a few known people who later came to this land carrying with them the demons of their past suffering, multiplying the hurt and desperately looking for healing at the same time. Their experiences were parts of an important process that continuously goes on in this land. The images of those people are only a few visible portrayals connected by invisible threads to the memories of many people in the past and many people in the present. Now you need to hear about some other people who worked in this land to consciously heal the suffering and to keep the fire of the great goddess Anakhita alive through their work.

"This place," Michael gestured to the site of the museum, "used to be a physical building, an opening to other spaces through which much hurt was transformed. It was built for this purpose by Ulugh Beg. It was his observatory. His father made him a ruler of Samarkand when he was still a teenager. He was an empowered being, initiated into the ancient knowledge of this land. This is his museum. It was built on the place where the remains of his star observatory were uncovered."

Michael moved to the right, so I got up from the bench, as he looked like he was going to show me something. On the other side of the museum, we reached a big crater in the ground with metal rails circling it. The rails were what remained of a huge circle which could have supported the movement of some large body through the large diameter of the man-made crater.

"That's all that was left," said Michael in a reserved voice. "He was a ruler of Samarkand for forty years. His grandfather was Timur, another one of those three warriors I told you about at the beginning of our talks. You see, we have quite different memories of history here from what you have in the West. You remembered Alexander as the Great; we remember him as the Horrible. You know

Timur as Tamerlane, the lame monster who brought terror wherever he went. We remember him as the great master who returned life to Samarkand and its people. In both
perspectives, you can see the gaps in the collective memory, kept opposite to each other, rejecting each other. But
these gaps hurt the memories of our ancestors and still
hurt ours.

"Timur was trying to relieve the memory demons he
generated through his war campaigns by building beautiful temples in Samarkand. He was sealing his memory by
turning horror into beauty, and he achieved high skills in
that art. But one of his own gaps was his announcement
that he was related to Genghis Khan, the one who tortured
this city two hundred years before him. Along with the
power of Genghis Khan's name, Timur had to accept
Khan's disturbed memories. He did, and he was finding
ways to deal with them. When he was ready to die, he
knew that his going into the ground had to be careful,
because his memory was connected to this land and he
wanted to be buried in a special way to protect this land
from his fears and traumas.

"His body was taken back to his golden city, Samarkand,
from far away, from a remote place in the north where he
had died suddenly. He had been preparing to invade China
after he had conquered most of Asia. His grandson, ten-
year-old Ulugh Beg, was with Timur in his camp. By that
time, he had already seen a few battles with his grandfather. Nobody knows what the dying Timur told his grandson, but he didn't pass onto Ulugh Beg his unhealed fears
and unresolved memories; he took them to his grave. Ulugh
Beg brought his grandfather's body to Samarkand, and
Timur was buried in a mausoleum in Gur Amir. One thing
he took care of before dying was to give instructions to not
disturb his grave, saying it might be dangerous for the living. He knew what horror he was taking into the earth with
him, and he didn't want it to come back.

"In the beginning of the twentieth century, a Russian scientist, Vyatkin, found this place where the observatory used to be. He did a lot of digging around Afrasiab but didn't leave much information of what he had found. The observatory ruins were one of the few sites he described; the rest of his material disappeared at the time of his death.

"You know when they opened Timur's grave for the first time? The Soviet scientist Gerasimov, who was obsessed with the reconstruction of facial features from scalp remains, came here with permission of the Soviet government and opened Timur's grave to reconstruct his face. No one here would do that because they remembered Timur's warning, but the Soviet scientist did it anyway. He opened the grave on June 22, 1941, a few hours before the war with Germany was announced in the Soviet Union. Timur's foreshadowing came true."

"Why was it difficult to find the observatory if most of the buildings in Samarkand from the time of Timur were well preserved?"

"Because it was destroyed." Michael's face darkened as if an invisible cloud had gone over it. "It was leveled not by foreign invasion, but by our own creatures of fear who knew that Ulugh Beg's work was taking away power from them. The observatory he had built didn't have any peers in the world. It was a three-story, round building, constructed to facilitate a connection to the stars. You can read about Ulugh Beg's scientific achievements; they were brilliant, but his psychological work remains unknown. I told you that the people here were the big dreamers, that they worked with the substance of death and dreams, and that they preserved powerful ways of transformation. The work performed here was aimed at making immortality available to as many people as possible.

"It was a science that used a profound knowledge of the process of dying and of preserving the individual awareness after that. The connection with stars was involved in this. Ulugh Beg's observatory had drawings of seven stars on its inner walls considered to be the gates for transformation. Those were the seven gates opening the way to seven different types of afterlife existence.

"Our teachers from the past knew the different stages awareness goes through when the body dies. Fighting the memory demons is the first stage; its successful resolution is connected celestially with going through the Sun gate. This is a stage where most people have to face a second death and lose the chance of immortality because they forget who they are. They become terrified by their memory demons and lose the connection with the loving power of the Sun, which is always connected with our own heart and has the face of the goddess Anakhita."

When I heard Michael say those words, I immediately remembered the experience with the stone sculpture that he generated for me in the Gypsy camp.

"That second face on the chest of the sculpture that I saw in the tent, is it connected with what you are saying now?"

"It showed exactly that. This image is usually called the god Zurvan, the god known to people as the main god of Time and Death. But Zurvan is a later mask that the goddess Anakhita accepted to protect her face and to preserve her power. It is her face that is reflected in our own heart. It is her face that gives us the ultimate refuge from any hurtful memories and from the guilt, fear, worry, and sadness they cause. She grants us salvation from the second death when we know how to connect with her in the first transformational stage following the physical death. After that is accomplished, individual awareness goes through the next stage of passing through one of the seven star gates. It becomes attracted to one of those seven star gates, depending on what type of future experience is needed. The choice of one of seven stars defines the fate of one's afterlife.

"Much knowledge was gathered here and made public by Ulugh Beg for the first time since the Golden Time. But he himself had to be prepared for sacrifice. He knew that the demons collected in the memories of people, including his family line, were too strong and sooner or later would try to destroy him. The legend says that the line of Shahrukh, Ulugh Beg's father, was damned after Shahrukh executed a few holy men in the mountains during one of his war campaigns. Ulugh Beg knew about the danger coming to him from his ancestor's deeds. He secretly prepared a special refuge for himself in case of his untimely death.

"He completed most of the sacred buildings in Samarkand, and in one of them he chose to protect himself after death from the memory demons, so they wouldn't be able to distort the memory of him and wouldn't interfere with his afterlife transformation. He prepared a secret tomb to undergo afterlife transformation. I know that place but I can't name it for you. It is still secret, and very powerful. And that place is different from what is now known as the official tomb of Ulugh Beg in Gur Amir.

"So, he was ready when death finally reached him. He was traveling, dressed in white, surrounded by the group of close pupils, when a sword blade cut through his neck. In one move it cut off his head from left to right, killing him in an instant. The murderer was hired by Ulugh Beg's son, Abd al-Latif, whose blood was open to the poison of Zaratashta's jealousy. Remember how memory demons recreate themselves through generating the hurt. Abd al-Latif himself was murdered a few months after his father's assassination. The night before his death, he saw his own head presented to him on a platter. The revenge reached him from inside first, from his own dreams, and he couldn't escape it. Soon after his death, his severed head was displayed over the entrance arch of Ulugh Beg's *madrasa*, the academy he built in Samarkand. The same fate was prepared for his descendants. Both Abd al-Latif's son and grandson met the same death.

"After Ulugh Beg's death, his enemies destroyed the observatory, smashed it to the ground, stating that it was a house of forty powerful evil spirits."

Michael grew silent and stood there still for a while with his widely open eyes fixed on the horizon, and he seemed to be enchanted with the images of his inner vision. Then he shook his head slightly and looked at me, saying in a regular voice, "I needed to tell you this story because telling it brings changes to the consequences of those remote events that continue influencing people in our time.

"I have told you what I could. It's been a long day. Now I need to go and to do some other things. I have a meeting in half an hour. And you need your rest now. It will be a long day tomorrow, your last day with me, and it will be a time for you to do what you promised at the very beginning: a healing for someone. Meet me tomorrow in the bazaar."

Chapter 12

There were not many people at the bazaar the next morning, and I saw Michael right away. He stood behind the rows of carpets, talking with tenderness to an old woman. She was of small stature and hardly reached Michael's shoulder. When they saw me coming, they turned toward me and started to talk to each other animatedly, obviously discussing me. I didn't feel uncomfortable about this at all. I felt throughout my body how much less fear it contained now and how I felt very light.

The woman looked into my face, smiling. Her face was deeply wrinkled, but her eyes—black, deep, and almond-shaped—were almost younger than Michael's, and laughter radiated from her face.

"This is my grandmother, Sulema," said Michael, and his voice was full of barely withheld laughter.

Through the reverence I felt immediately toward this small woman, I understood how much Michael meant to me, and how much respect I felt toward him.

"It is an honor to meet you," I said to her, and bowed my head slightly. They burst out laughing at this.

"Come to visit us," she said in a melodic, deep voice. "Come to our house with me. Michael will come later. He needs to buy herbs."

I walked with Sulema for a few blocks from the bazaar. The day was bright and the morning sun felt soft. The flowers filled the air with sweet scents. People were smiling at me, and I felt a joy walking with this woman through the old streets of Samarkand.

She turned a corner, and on a narrow street framed by a large tree was a small adobe house behind a white fence.

"Come in. We have some work to do," said Sulema, and unlocked the door with a large metal key.

She took me through the cool darkness of a few rooms straight to the backyard. The house reminded me of my grandmother's house in Russia: old, warm, welcoming, and protecting. There was a fireplace in the center of the backyard. The fire was still smoldering in it, and Sulema placed a few dried branches in it to make it larger. Old white bricks placed in a circle were a foundation. When Sulema moved around, taking large pots from the house to the wooden table outside, she looked like an ordinary grandmother, dressed in a dark, cotton dress. Somehow this was surprising for me, as if I already had decided that everything related to Michael should be extraordinary. But then, as if to prove my thought, she looked at me silently for a few moments and I sensed the presence of an extraordinary power. At those moments, I felt serious and focused. "Michael lived in this house since he was ten years old." She was probably sensing that any details of his life had significance for me now, and I listened carefully, trying not to ask questions or stop the flow of her talk.

"I thought I lost him before that. They went to live in Afghanistan, he and his parents. I saw him last when he was six. They sent back pictures, of course. But what can you say through pictures about how a child grows? Not much. I missed him so. But I knew that one day he would come back. I just didn't know that that day would be so painful. His mother and father had an important job to do in Afghanistan. I could only get news from them through the mail. I don't have a phone, you see. But one day a man knocked at my door. He had a large envelope. I was surprised they would send a letter not through the mail, as they did before, but by messenger. But the letter was not from them. It was about them. About the bomb that blew up the place where they worked and killed everybody there.

"The man said, 'My condolences,' and left. And I didn't even ask him about Michael. The letter said the family had been killed, and I knew in my heart that his mother and father had died. I knew it because I could mourn them. But I couldn't mourn Michael. I just couldn't. The only thing I could do was wait for him. I didn't ask anyone, didn't send any letters.

"One day, it was spring, like now, I heard that a Gypsy band had stopped in the city. I went to the bazaar and saw their circus. They were really good. Brave and funny. When I came home, I felt I couldn't wait for Michael anymore. I knew my heart couldn't take it any longer. It was that day when an old Gypsy man knocked at my door, and when I opened it I saw Michael standing with him at the doorstep. He didn't want to let go of the Gypsy's hand. His face was tanned, and so serious. But I saw that he had made peace with his parents' death. The Gypsies had healed him well. He had lived and traveled with them for more than a year. They picked him up in Afghanistan and healed him of his wounds. It was hard for a while after they left him with me.

"He never talked to me about his wandering with the Gypsies, but I am sure he remembers every detail. He would just mention a man once in a while and call him

'Grandfather.' But I know for sure that he wasn't my husband, that Gypsy grandfather." Sulema laughed again and took a brown cup, wiped it with clean linen, and handed it to me.

"I would treat you with my *plov*. I think I can say that I make the best *plov*, at least in this neighborhood." She looked around with laughter in her bright eyes, as if checking if anybody heard her. "But you are not supposed to eat before taking the drink."

"What does Michael do now? Did he finish school?"

Sulema laughed. "He could be a professor if he wanted to. He studied chemistry and astronomy at the university. Do you Russians think that everybody here is illiterate? Okay, okay, I know you don't. But many of your countrymen think that. Some of my countrymen would think it's the opposite," and she laughed benignly again. "What does he do now? I thought he told you. Magic is everything he lives for. He was educated in our clan after he came back from traveling. How he does it, you need to hear from him. But one thing I know is that he stays in this world to help me out in my older years. Me and that Gypsy grandfather of his, whom he still sees.

"Here he is," she announced cheerfully, and looking to my right I saw Michael standing in the doorstep at the entrance to the backyard. His well-proportioned, tall figure almost filled the entrance. Motionless, his head slightly pulled back, his arms relaxed at his side, his pose radiated such a harmony of his physical patterns that he looked like a perfect picture that had come alive by some miracle. He stood there in silence for some time. Then he turned his eyes toward me, and the moment I met his gaze an intense wave of sadness went through my body and I felt almost ready to cry.

It wasn't a personal feeling. After these days I had spent close to him, I still didn't know him "personally." Most things about him remained a mystery for me, and I didn't want to destroy that mystery. But again, his presence caused an intense feeling in me. I didn't completely understand the source of it, but felt that part of it was connected with realizing that very soon I would have to leave him. I knew that nowhere else would I encounter again the presence I felt within him, the ultimate presence of being. It was something I had never before met. I knew I would miss the way he experienced himself and those around him.

"I told you to get used to seeing me at the first meeting," he said. "You didn't listen, of course. That's why you feel this way now. Sadness is a price for the acceleration of experience. When you feel sad about something, you accept it faster. One of the functions of depression is to assist in acceptance of an experience, which otherwise remains foreign for the self and stays occupied by memory demons."

Michael moved around the fireplace and sat near me on an old blanket thrown to the ground near the fireplace.

"I asked you to work with the swastika to help clear the space of your dreams. It did help you. You may not consciously remember all the experiences the swastika's influence brought to your dreams, but your internal space is much more balanced and open now. Helping you clear your dream space was one of the ways to help you become ready to obtain knowledge from this place. Much of this knowledge is not only connected to the dream space, but was intentionally stored in it.

"The major task for our dreams is to fill in the gaps in our memory. The problem is that when the memory demons have populated your memory already, they will do everything to protect their existence. The problem is that they are much more alive, active, and powerful in dreams than in waking life. So, unfortunately, when the dream space is not clear, quite often instead of healing, the dream brings an intensification of the hurt of the trauma. To beat them up, the memory demons, you have to be equipped with knowledge that can allow you to work inside the dream. It is worth the effort, since complete healing happens through changing the structure of the images, not simply their meanings. That is easier to do through working with dreams.

"It is more difficult to alter your waking patterns which are held mostly by beliefs implanted in you while you're growing up. Beliefs which tell you bluntly what is right and wrong, what deserves praise and what deserves punishment. In dreams, it is so much easier because dreams don't allow separation of wholeness into good and bad, right and wrong. It is against their nature. In dreams, everything is allowed.

"Now, use a little introspection and tell me what has been the main change in the quality of your dreams since you have been here?"

It was a hard question to answer. Mainly because my experience in Samarkand was so different, so unusual, it all felt like one amazing dream. I tried to concentrate and then told Michael, "I would say it was the way in which I started to experience myself in the dream. I began to experience the one who is seeing the dream much more strongly. The dreams I have had during the last few nights have been intense and diverse. It would be hard to cite the details. But I would say that the main change was that the sense of self which I felt behind all that dream imagery was much more present and strong."

"Can you try to remember it now?"

I saw how Sulema stopped on the other side of the fireplace and looked at me with that same intensity in her eyes, waiting for me to reply.

"I don't know. I am not dreaming now."

"That's exactly what you need to reexperience. Look around, pay attention to every detail, and then make an effort in your mind to believe that everything you see—me, grandmother, the fire—all that is your dream which you are seeing right now. Reconstruct the feeling."

"But I don't want to do it. I don't want to see you as just a dream."

"Olga, when will you trust me completely?" He smiled so gently that I felt something unnatural behind my resistance to follow his advice.

"This is one of the main mechanisms by which spirits of trauma keep their power over our memory. By making us believe that memory and dreams are not significant. It is *just* a dream, they make us think. This is an example of clever separation. The truth is that there is not any priority of one type of experience over another. Dreams are not less important. They are different, but they are part of the whole psyche. So, try to make an effort."

Saying this, Michael put his hand over my wrist, the same way he did on the first evening I saw him.

I looked around, and after what he had just said, it was easy to remember the sense of being inside the dream. There was not much difference between what I remembered as my night dreams and my experience in that moment. The tongues of fire on the ground grew slightly larger in the middle of the backyard, reinforced by a warm wind coming from outside the fence. Sulema, with the same expression of serious concentration, sat on the ground by the fireplace. I felt Michael's hand touching my skin, felt the warmth of sunlight on my face. Each of the sounds, colors, and sensations I experienced now was a different thread connecting my perception with the world. All these sensations were coming into my body through different channels and were being integrated into one in my heart, which was overfilled with a sweet, intense sensation.

"Now it's time for you to do the healing work," said Michael.

I had wondered this morning who I was supposed to work with. I didn't see any signs that we were waiting for somebody to come. I looked through the flames to Sulema, and decided it was probably her healing I was supposed to assist in. She smiled, but her smile didn't support my thought.

"It is not Sulema that you need to work for," said Michael, and took his hand off my wrist. That changed my perception slightly, but I still was able to keep the sense of remembering my dream self. "It is Lara you need to heal," he said.

I looked at him, astonished, trying to understand what he meant.

"It is only your mind that needs to give a meaning to what I said. But *you* already know what I mean because it is a natural continuation of what you have been experiencing these days. She exists in your memory, so through working with your memory you can produce real changes. I told you a few days ago that she is a live person and needs to be healed from the memory demon that took her over. I wasn't mistaken. I knew then that she had killed herself, but I also know that existence doesn't end with physical death. I don't believe it is ever too late to heal."

"But how? How, Michael, can I possibly do that?"

"What you are about to do, shamans would call walking the soul of the dead. You can call it transpersonal transformation or whatever name makes you less anxious. The process is still going to be the same. The process of transformation will only happen in the reality where internal and external spaces are the same, where there are no longer any mental boundaries separating them. It is not exactly a dream state. It is a particular state which you can enter when your dream space and your memory space are open and clear and you can move through them easily. It will be up to your memory to choose what images to create to generate the healing. Your memory images will be carriers of transformation, but the effect of the changes will extend beyond your personal memory. I am going to watch over you and to help you in moments when you may need it. To make it real, you will need to take this drink."

In his hands was that same brown cup Sulema had given me to hold. It now contained a viscous substance like milk mixed with crushed herbs.

"What is it?" Anxiety found its way back into my body.

"It is not a drug, if this is what you are afraid of. Drugs are one of the tools the spirits of trauma use to keep the hurt in place. We don't use them. It is a special herb that grows near the mountain north of here. Sulema prepared it with milk so it wouldn't be too bitter. The main thing it does is relax your muscles. It keeps you awake while you're dreaming, and at the same time it washes away all the tension knots in your muscles which are the bodily representations of your memory knots. So your memory becomes free for some time, and you are protected from your usual fears so you can experience your memories much more consciously than usual.

"Your experience will take its own special form. But the content of it will not be the main thing that matters. What matters is the process of change. And what matters is the process of finding the memory demon and conquering it to make it serve you and further healing in the future."

He handed me the warm cup, and I took it reluctantly. Then I put it on the ground, fear rippling through my body.

"Olga, when will you trust me completely?"

I looked at him again, and suddenly a new feeling overwhelmed me. The feeling that I had known him for ages, that his presence was something I knew so well long ago, but forgot, saying it was just a dream. The feeling was so strong, so authentic, that my fear became insignificant. I reached the point where I could trust him with my life.

I took the cup and drank its contents slowly. The creamy, milky taste soothed the bitterness of the herbs. Nothing changed.

The same warm wind was gently touching my skin. Sulema was still sitting in front of me, putting logs in the fire. I didn't see Michael but acutely felt his presence on my right side.

I didn't have any expectations. I was just sitting there, looking at the fire, which soon became the focus of my vision. Only Sulema's face on the other side of the fire was still visible to me. I heard her saying, "We love storytelling here. Can you tell me a story now? Tell me the most puzzling story you know." I thought Sulema asked me that just to help me feel more comfortable, and I was grateful to her for that.

"Now?"

"Sure, why not?"

I thought about her suggestion for a while, and then suddenly the story of Hamlet, a story that had been puzzling me since high school, came suddenly to my mind.

"All right. I know such a story. It has been puzzling me for years, since I never was able to find any final, complete, and unambiguous meaning to it. This story happened long ago.

"There was a prince who lived in a faraway land. His father had died recently. His mother married his uncle and the uncle became the king, and the prince lived in his kingdom. He wasn't a particularly sad prince and he wasn't particularly lonely. He definitely wasn't mad, until one day when everything changed and the prince began to change.

"That day, or more exactly that night, he met the ghost of his dead father, who told him a story of how the reigning king, his own brother, poisoned him to death to get the kingdom and the queen. His father's ghost demanded revenge, and there was no peace left for the prince after he learned that story. He invented a clever trick: he invited wandering actors to perform for the king and the queen with a play the prince had created himself. The play was the story of his father's murder, played out by actors before the prince's mother and his uncle. He saw the proof of guilt in their faces as they watched the play, and then he became truly mad."

"He was killed, right? The prince is killed at the end of the story, right?" Sulema interrupted me without waiting for me to finish.

"Actually, yes, he was. You know the story?"

"That ghost killed him, the ghost of his father."

"Actually, no . . ."

"Actually, yes. He started to play by the rules of the ghost. He let the spirit of trauma in, into himself, he allowed the demon to invade his memory with the hurt of his father's death and to become a part of himself. He started acting from the spirit's command, so he had to be killed. He didn't become mad, as you say. He was just fighting the spirit of trauma. He lost, I guess. He didn't have a wife, did he?"

"No. But he had a fiancée with whom he was very tender at first, but then she killed herself because of his rudeness and madness."

"Whoa! Were there more dead people in this story?"

"Actually, yes. The bride's father and . . ."

"Oh! A really hungry ghost he was, that father lookalike. That was a good story. The one who wrote it knew about the battle."

Sulema grew silent and her squinting eyes looked straight at me through the fire, as if she was seeing through me. I saw her kind smile through the flames until they rose up again and her face became hidden behind the fire.

I started to feel my bodily sensations change. It felt as if some invisible power penetrated my tensed muscles and untied the old painful knots stored in them. Along with that, I felt my memory was liberating and changing itself into the same substance of which dreams are made, and soon a stream of images was flowing through my mind. They flowed in abundance, but there was no chaos to it; they were connected by an invisible, profound order, and my perception followed this.

The fire kept moving slightly, but its shape now was perfectly round, as if the sun, by a miracle, were burning in front of me in a duplicate of itself. I stared at it for a while, until everything turned red, and the sun disk became black. I closed my eyes and felt how this little sun in front of me was pulsating and approaching me. I tried to stay still—very, very still—until I heard the noise, like a gate opening, and Michael said, "Fear nothing and remember that it is the father who punishes and it is the mother who forgives. I will be with you when you need me."

Chapter 13

My body is vibrating and growing. All the energy of tension stored in my body is suddenly released and the energy flows. My inner space expands. Air fills me up, and my body, solid and dense a minute ago, seems made of many wide, airy corridors which continued to expand. I could have never imagined before that so much space was contained inside me.

The interior corridors are alive and moving, and one of them grew bigger in an instant and pulled in all my attention, as if there was some magnet in it. I am pure space, white and open, and Michael's voice, somewhat muted, sounds in the center of it. I see him clearly nearby, in white clothes, his hair pulled back in a ponytail, sitting still, his arms crossed on his chest. He looks at me and I know that he knows what happened to me and what is about to happen, and I listen to him carefully.

"This is a land of your memory. It is as real as a land of your home country. It can be very deceptive so you need to keep your intention to go forward firm, no matter what. Move through this space and fear nothing."

At first I see a long passageway, a narrow, gray tunnel. Two high, heavy stone blocks covered in some places by fresh, green, lush moss fix the limits of this narrow corridor. A dim blue light comes to it from only one direction, above, and it is difficult to see the ground. I lift my head and see, right above me, straight rows of vertical tubes hanging down from the ceiling. Light is oozing through their tubular openings, and with fear I realize that these are human bones made to serve as lamps for this corridor.

There are hundreds of them placed near each other, and they move slightly above my head, the blue-gray light moving with them as I walk through. Sometimes their moves create a sound reminding me of heavy sighs. I don't have time to get used to them because the scene changes and the bone lamps disappear unexpectedly. I walk through the next corridor which is lit from its sides. I can't see the source of light, for it is hidden behind old, washed-out, gray-white sheets which serve as walls for this corridor. These sheets separate me from masses of moving bodies behind them. I don't know whether these beings milling about behind the fabric are humans or large animals. There is no way to tell by the sounds they make. They don't talk. They just breathe heavily, sniffling and tossing and turning, pushing each other, so close to me, so nearby.

I feel that there are hundreds of them stuck in that tiny space behind the sheets, and I feel they know about me walking through. They feel my presence as acutely as I feel theirs. Sometimes their large limbs are pushed by another body and they touch me through the dirty sheet as I walk past. The round waves of their movements, which somehow I know they are trying to hold back while I walk near them, coincide with the waves of nausea I feel. I hurry my steps.

I almost see the exit from this horrible gallery and try to reach it as soon as I can. And at the same time, I know I must not run. I feel in every cell of my skin that the minute I run, they will pass through the sheets, and nothing will hold back their movements, and they will smash me instantly with their huge, heavy bodies. I keep walking fast. The next moment, it is finished, and with a sigh of relief I leave the corridor and walk into a large hall.

The heavy background rhythm and sniffling of the moving bodies behind me merges into a rhythmic, mechanical noise filling this new room. I don't see any figures at first. The room reminds me of an abandoned industrial building, with high ceilings and cement floors; all the workers have left, leaving their machines still running. Chaos rules here: broken wooden frames, shattered glass that crunches under my feet, the squeaks of rats running somewhere through piles of paper tossed into the corner. The room is full of signs of decay, but the background mechanical sound stays constant, indicating that something is kept going.

I walk carefully through the piles of old broken things. I stumble upon the remains of furniture, shredded, yellowing newspapers printed in a foreign language. Here and there, I have to turn to be able to pass through all this garbage overfilling the room. A light wind touches my skin from time to time, making me think that there must be a door or window open in the room to allow air to circulate. When I move almost to the middle of the hall, I see that the source of this wind and of the constant mechanical noise is a giant, dark wooden mill. I can't understand why I didn't notice it before; it is so huge I can't see its top, high up at the unreachable ceiling. The mill vibrates constantly and generates a mechanical, irritating noise. This vibration is being accumulated in the mill to prepare it to make a giant turn. A sinister groan comes from somewhere around me, as if this sound was created by an unbearable pain.

My body freezes in a terror that doesn't allow me to move. I lower my eyes without turning my head. The next scene shocks me to the very depths of my being, and the terror I felt a second ago is as nothing compared to the horror I now feel in me and around me. Broken pieces I took for the remains of furniture change their appearance, and they are human limbs and parts of corpses thrown around everywhere. They are alive. They move. Some of them are trying to crawl.

The groan I heard a moment before is produced by them as proof of their extreme suffering. I see an upside-down human leg; the knee is being eaten by a black rat near me. It intentionally tortures the human flesh with its disgusting teeth. The leg itself has a human form only as far as the ankle, beyond which, the skin and muscles and bones are attached to iron figures.

Fighting an attack of nausea, I see more human parts with the iron figures of animals fixed to them as if by somebody's wild imagination. They try to crawl, but the iron is very heavy. I feel that it would be so safe and attractive to accelerate my fear and discomfort to the maximum degree and make my consciousness faint to stop seeing these revolting images. But when I feel the cold sweat across my body and saliva filling my mouth, signaling I'm closer to the saving collapse, I remember the rule I promised to keep. Fear nothing. I can't use the escape of losing consciousness. I have to look at the fear. I have to experience it. I agreed to this at the beginning, so I have to experience it in full. My nausea gets weaker, and my vision clears.

A loud, high-pitched whistle comes from somewhere above. The giant mill begins its turn. Before my panic makes me run, I notice with relief that the blades of the mill are rays of light. They're bright and intense, but they're still only light. So I stay where I am, without feeling any danger. When the wide blade of moving light touches me, I feel nothing different from the usual touch sunlight makes on my skin on a warm day.

However, this is not the case for the human remains around me. At the first sign of the turning mill, they become desperate, trying to free themselves from the burden of the iron animals, and their howls and groans blend into one unearthly cry that shakes the heavy walls of the room.

The ray-blades go through them slowly, lighting them up one after another. In one instant, the iron animal figures touched by this turning light are made red-hot as this fire impulse goes through them, striking the human flesh connected to them and creating burning pain. These animals pulsate the pain through the limbs. I suddenly feel so sorry for these human remains. I never thought one could feel sorry toward severed human parts, but my heart almost stops when I feel the pain going through their still-human cells. These limbs don't have personalities; they are not associated with faces; the groans they make are not human. They are the screams of tormented flesh.

I feel sadness for those screaming human parts. These images are entering my memory to stay for a long time.

I turn away from the grinding mill, though without much hope of getting relief from the sadness. Next, I see a huge cavity, as if somebody's throat had been magnified many times, but separated from its body, hung by a few threads from the ceiling. I see a red, inflamed mucous membrane as if this mouth were open wide to scream. But the scream can't come out because it is filled with a sharp razor, which goes back and forth through this piece of flesh, somehow without cutting it to pieces, but only causing pain.

This is too much to bear. I can't be on my own anymore. I need to hear Michael's voice and know he is with me.

"Michael, why do I see this? Why do I have to see this?"

I hear him answering, "To make yourself feel better, just remember it is not the content and form that matters but the process of change. What you are experiencing sometimes is called the Hall of Separation. It is not the first place human attention can go after death. There are hundreds of different pathways of experience through which the individuality of a person who died can go.

"What you see here are remains of human forms and therefore the remains of human individual attention, because attention and form are highly connected. For most humans who stay untrained and uneducated during their lives about existence after death, the process of the physical body's destruction is accompanied by the destruction of individual awareness. Don't mistake awareness for soul. When you are told by spiritual traditions that the soul is eternally alive and infinitely present, that is true. But how many people know their souls during their lives? How many of them are able to identify their souls? Only a few. For the rest, regular awareness of the body is the seat of attention, and individual awareness goes through disintegration along with the body.

"Since the ancient Mysteries which taught the practice of healing in the afterlife and the correct transfer of consciousness to the afterlife are now forgotten or hidden, the majority of people dying have to endure a very painful process of dismemberment by the demons of their memories. What you see in this room is the final stage of such disintegration, when sensations have been separated from memory, feelings from thoughts, faces from members. You meet on this final stage the essential manifestations of those sensations.

"In the case of this hall, the sensation is pain. You have to go through this hall to reach your goal. But there are other halls where different sensations are experienced. Don't be confused by your reason. The suffering you saw is not connected to a particular person anymore. But it has an individualized nature. It has to do with what their attention was mostly tuned to during their lives.

"These are the physical 'islands of memories,' parts of the body which memory demons used to live in. Your culture would call it punishment for sins. The main attribute of sin, if we are to use this term at all, is not its moral characteristic, but its ability to stop further development, to block further movement. All 'great' sinners, as essentially the personifications of the memory demons and whatever wrong deeds they did, had one thing in common: their awareness was fixed on the *subject* of their sin, be it greed, lust, jealousy, or anger.

"These different qualities served as a dam built up against their development and transformation. And this is what started the process of segregation and involution. When they died and disintegration began, their awareness was stuck with only their sin and trauma, and they died a second death, losing their individual awareness eventually. Their individual selves ceased their existence after the second death."

I look around, trying to correlate the words I heard with the images I see. Severed body parts and a horrible sense of suffering interfere with my thinking. I can't come to any conclusion, but I know that the words I heard have entered my consciousness, and sooner or later they will come back to me, and I will understand them better.

Only now I notice that the air in this room has a particular dense quality, denser than the air I am used to breathing. Or maybe my distorted sense of gravity creates this illusion of dense air. Some objects levitate slowly, lifting up from the floor to hang in space. I see a strange figure approaching, making efforts to fly toward me through this dense air. It is a human with the face of a young man, but the face is distorted by his enormous physical labor to get closer to me. He hangs in the air, his body only a torso and head. His limbs are absent and he wriggles to move through the air.

I am afraid to say anything or to make him talk, for he is repulsive and I don't even want to think about him talking to me. But he is closing in on me with a definite intention to communicate. I hold myself still, even though the temptation to run away is strong.

He floats right in front of me now. I see his face clearly. His features are regular and thin, distorted by constant suffering and anger as marked in the deep wrinkles across his face.

He makes nervous facial movements while looking at me with irritation. Even with its numerous wrinkles, this face still belongs to a fairly young man in his forties. His light brown hair is shaved short, and with a little imaginative effort I can see him as a normal man who would have probably worn a long black coat, been competitive in his career, and lived in a fancy Manhattan apartment. This picture helps me to adjust to the prospect of talking to him.

So with a little reticence, I dare to ask him, just to stop that unblinking look with which he stares at me, "Who are you?"

"I am the one who tries to stay a human being." His voice sounds more sad than angry, which makes me feel more at ease. "But it's not easy, as you can see," he adds with unhidden irony. "I went away unprepared. I was walking to have a lunch with a very important partner when the siren of a police car got very close, and I heard a few shots nearby. I know I died then but still don't have any idea if I was shot or run over by a speeding car."

The way he speaks about his interrupted lunch is strange, as if he still regretted that he had lost that business opportunity. But I keep listening.

"You know that I can't tell you how I came to a realization of my death. And even if it were permitted, I would never do it myself, for the fear and horror that came along with it are too harrowing to recall. I tell you only that nothing I thought in my short life about my possible end proved to be true. I never believed in anything beyond that life and found it ridiculous to spend my time and energy in thinking about such an abstract thing as dying. How ridiculous. No eternal dream, no infinite darkness, no instant disappearance were granted me.

"I had to endure thousands of years of wondering, searching, and fighting, and I am not exaggerating—I really felt it to be that long. Finally, here I am, stuck in the place of pain and degradation, the permanent industry in the middle of a kingdom of pain. Why am I here? What for? I don't have any idea. The only thing I know is that after those years of my mortal experiences, I am forced to give up my human identity, and to let my body parts go and suffer each on their own. But I am not going to let it happen. I am going to fight those suckers, and I am going to win! Do you hear me?! Do you hear me, you stupid nothing, thinking of yourself as a center of everything? I don't give a damn about your intentions! I will have my body, whatever it costs, and I am going to win, you loser!"

He screams hysterically, seemingly at nowhere, for the room stays the same, the mechanical noise keeps going, and nothing notices his presence except me. Then his face softens, his lips tremble, and desperate tears pour down his cheeks. Ironically, he has no hands to wipe them away.

I feel I am almost crying with him. I can't understand why this man is undergoing such suffering. I reach out my hand and wipe away his tears, feeling the soft, cool skin of his hollow cheeks. He sighs heavily and grows calm. He thanks me with a slight nod of his head, still trying to fight his tears. And then I turn around and say into the space of the room, "Why? Why does he have to endure this?"

But instead of coming to me, the answer is addressed to him. He can hear it, and, in fact, he listens to it with passion.

"You, Victor, do not understand much about yourself. You never took the reality of your soul to be as serious as some stupid business lunch you still care about. All the things that have been happening to you are mere attempts to turn your attention and to help you finally to realize yourself. What you are fighting for is not the real you but just some image you are used to thinking of as yourself. Don't hold onto it; let it go. You have all the potential to realize the truth now, so don't put yourself through suffering anymore. And it's not your fault. You are the product of the time into which you were born.

"You were a being with no sense of real self or real freedom, stuck between the ideas and ideals of people around you, trying to fit into them and going ever farther away from yourself and *your* goals. That's why you never learned any tools to change things other than anger and hatred. You despised violence in your city, but never knew anything better than to hate those committing it. You were tired and exhausted by the endless competition in your job, but didn't have any means to deal with it other than to become more and more angry and to continue to hurt. You were an ignorant human being, but it wasn't your fault really.

"You can experience a different fate. You just need to see it and to accept it. It's difficult, for you were trained all your life that to be soft and compassionate is almost equal to being a loser, the one thing you never wanted to be. But that time is over. Turn around now. Look at these human remains. Try to feel that there are human fates associated with them, as well as mistakes, suffering, hurt, unforgiveness. Try to feel your compassion. The minute you feel it, you will forget your illusory battle."

Victor's face softens, relaxes. Tears roll once again down his cheeks, but these tears are different. He is being transformed into a gentle, sweet being. The voice continues talking to him.

"Follow me now. You were able to change your vision, so your experience can now change, too. Follow me."

Victor obviously sees his guide, who for me is only a voice. The voice doesn't sound like Michael, but I don't have time to pay more attention to recognizing it. Victor moves through the air to the end of this room and then goes out through a massive iron door which opens when he approaches. I follow him, trying to keep up with his easy flight. I walk fast, and with no regret leave the saddest room I've ever visited.

We stand now at the shore of a blue lake. It is not big, but its clear, crystalline water reveals no bottom. Victor sits his handicapped body near the lake. His face looks enlightened, his deep wrinkles almost dissolved.

I hear him saying quietly, "This is the first time since my death that I have heard my name pronounced."

"You are being granted release," his guide continues. "This is a lake of forgetfulness. This is the highest release that can be granted to you now. You've endured a long journey to reach it. But it was always nearby, from the very moment when the car of that drunk driver ran you over. It was all in your mind, your own pattern of resistance and fighting back, that kept you walking from one space to another, endlessly seeking victory in a fight nobody had with you but yourself. Drink this water and dissolve your memory in it. Give it all back and be free. That's the maximum mercy that is being given to you, for you never strove for anything else and never learned how to progress beyond it. Go ahead and do it. Good-bye, Victor."

Victor smiles kindly, and his lips whisper a long-awaited "thank you." He moves his body closer to the water and lowers his face toward it.

Then he drinks the water in greedy gulps. The crystalline liquid enters his body, flows gently inside. It fills him up, cleaning and washing out his body, dissolving its tangibility, thinning his contours, making him more subtle, until I see only clear blue water that still holds the shape of his body. Then, in a slight wave, it pushes itself into the lake and merges with its water. And, as if a slight wind passed through the shore, I hear his final sigh, and the water in the lake becomes still and smooth again.

I stand there, fascinated by this miracle. I feel such an attraction to this lake, which appears capable of resolving suffering so gracefully, that I can't keep myself from reaching out my hand to touch its gentle waters with gratitude.

"Don't you dare do it." It is certainly Michael's voice. He sounds almost angry. "You are not supposed to touch it. Don't do it, please," he repeats more softly when I pull myself away from the shore. "You don't have much time left. Hurry up, if you want to accomplish your task."

Chapter 14

Next, I find myself in front of a metal door in the middle of a stone wall. The door is shorter than me, so I bend my head to enter when it opens. It does so with a tight, rusted squeak, indicating that it been closed for ages.

"Hello. How are you?" I can't hold myself back from making this greeting toward a small strange animal in the room. It looks as if it has been waiting for me for a long time and is exhausted and nervous because of that, even though it seems ready to run ahead of me, showing me the way.

It is a strange combination: part small, black dog with a long tail and part unknown animal whose head tops this strange creature. The head is small in proportion to the body and resembles a bird with a long beak that looks soft and strong at the same time. I am not afraid of this animal. Its friendly intentions are present in its every quick movement.

It is impatient, ready to leave, but as soon as I intend to follow it, an unexpected obstacle reveals itself. The flat iron plates that almost completely cover the floor suddenly rise up with a whistle and crashing sound. Two massive iron horses appear, so large they almost fill the room. Their thin, long necks are topped by very small heads with massive iron beaks. These monsters raise themselves up from the floor with unbelievable speed, transform themselves from flat plates into three-dimensional bodies, and face each other with all their unimaginable strength, crashing their heads into each other, sparks flying from their clashing beaks. The next instant, they fall down as rapidly as they arose and lie on the floor as lifeless pieces of iron again.

I understand at once that there is no way left for me to pass through this room. I know that any slight movement near these horses will wake them again and make them crush with their iron beaks anything that would try to cross their territory. As a proof of my guess, these giants jump up again, sparked by the slight movement of an insect. For a moment I feel lost. I know there is no way back for me, that I can't return the way I came. At the same time, I see no ways to avoid the iron beaks and pass through the room.

I stay motionless, not knowing what to do, when my attention is attracted by the jumping of the small black animal. These unrestrained jumps cause no reaction from the sleeping iron guards and the animal can freely jump back and forth between their now-passive beaks. The animal looks at me with clever eyes, which themselves seem to be jumping. I begin to understand that if I can allow my body to copy exactly its pattern of movements, then I will be unnoticed by the guardians too.

I study the whirling dog, trying to catch the essence of its movements. Then I realize that what makes those movements so specific, and what makes him invulnerable in the present situation, is their pure playfulness. The animal doesn't care. Every muscle in its body sends out a signal saying it doesn't care what happens to its body. It fears nothing and its carefree, flexible, impatient body says this.

I associate easily with this impatience. My destination is still far away and is more important to me than anything else, and this helps me let go of my fear and start moving. Initially, I try to move at a safe distance from the sleeping horses. But the dog's cheerful acceptance of my movements, half-dance, half-march, excites me and I move more freely, approaching the sleeping iron figures almost without noticing. The animal takes it as a game and dares me farther into the center of the room. I don't hear any sound coming from it, but I am sure that it laughs in its own way, and that this laughter and carefreeness gets transferred to me. At some point, I forget about the iron danger and just run after this animal who irritates me on purpose, who runs faster and faster, slipping away from me every time my hands are ready to catch it.

Then a horrible crash behind my back freezes me where I stand and without turning my head I know, with a sense of horror, that those horses are crashing behind me. Yet I am filled with relief from the thought that I am out of their reach. I can keep walking ahead and forget about them as something from a nightmare. The animal runs in front of me and I follow it to the next room.

I feel this is a place where I am supposed to do something important and do it quickly. I sense my time in this place is limited and I have to use it wisely to complete everything. The room reminds me of an art gallery I visited once in Santa Fe, New Mexico, where the owner was going out of business. He was running around the shop, his pictures and sculptures in disarray on the floor and against the walls. He was trying to save something from the chaos the capricious tourist market had thrown him into. No owner is visible in this room now. Old heavy frames, some wooden, some of blackened metal, hold paintings and stand against the wall, one leaning on the other in such a way that I can see only frames, not the paintings.

Without thinking, just following an urgent feeling which prompts me, I walk toward the paintings, sorting out frames without looking at the pictures. But my peripheral vision is active, as always happens when I allow myself to experience the guidance of intuition, and I see the contours of faces, and the realization comes that my hands are leafing through portraits.

Somehow I know that this trembling feeling in my hands can be caused only by the presence of Lara's face still hidden on a canvas. I pull a silver frame out. It's heavy with intricate decorations, and the canvas is partially torn. I don't look at it and I feel no temptation to do so. It is clear that looking at the portrait is prohibited, and I don't mind. I take it into my hands to decide what to do next.

I know there is no way I am going to leave Lara's portrait in this endless row of faces. I take it as far away from the wall as I can and look for help. The frame is too heavy for me to carry. My small black animal is near me again and, by signs, makes me look to my right, where I notice a donkey. He looks at me with his big, somewhat surprised eyes and waits for me to use him as a support for the picture.

I place the frame carefully on the donkey's back and, steadying it, we quickly leave the room. We walk through an open space into a forest. Walking through this forest is so refreshing that I don't mind that our walk is a long one and that I can't see the end of it on the horizon. I try to understand the significance of this passage, for I can't help noticing the different quality of the air in the forest, the particular combination of sounds surrounding us which I can't associate with any forest sounds I have heard before. The light here is special too, and comes through the trees in a way I haven't seen in any other forests. I try to figure out what is so special about this path and why it feels so important to move through it.

I feel Michael's presence strongly again, as if he is walking near me. I feel I am in a separate stream of my dream where I can't see him, but he can see me and know everything that is happening to me.

Then I hear him saying, "It's not a mere forest you are moving through. It is a land of transition. It may look like a forest to one person, but to another it might be presented as a river or a mighty, endless ocean. The form it takes is subjective. The form doesn't matter, as I told you. Whatever personal consciousness is ready to perceive, that is what is shown to it.

"The significance of this passage comes from its position of being a bridge between different 'rooms' and 'corridors' where particular qualities of human nature are being worked out. There are endless varieties of those rooms where this or that quality is presented to individual awareness to test its affiliation with it. If part of a person's memory was too occupied with those qualities and wasn't integrated with the rest of the psyche, the chance is high that one will lose oneself to the memory demons in one of the rooms, and one's evolution and release will be delayed for a long time.

"Passages like this forest have a great advantage. They are tunnels connecting different dimensions, and as such, they possess the highest potential to liberate the dead from endless wandering and to help them enter the next stage of the afterlife. It is quite difficult to do this because the fear of death is the final basic fear into which all other possible fears can be incorporated the way pieces of a puzzle can yield a completed picture after they have been put together. Every fear other than the fear of death, however gigantic and total it may seem at the moment of its experience, is always partial, is always a piece of the puzzle. It always indicates the presence of some boundary, some crossroad. People experience fear every time they reach a line of demarcation between different states, and fear is the basic reaction to the possibility of a change of state. The fear of death is always the last fear. It grabs you not with anticipation of death, but inside death itself.

"Lara was brave, but when she entered dying, she wasn't ready for that ultimate fear. The more one has these gaps filled with fears, the more difficult it becomes to achieve liberation in the afterlife. You have realized that the first gap which created your relation to Lara and defined your actions in the past was that 'Good women can't be raped.' That was your first gap as much as it was hers, and it kept destroying her memory. Now it's time to learn about the second gap.

"It is your belief that suicide is a sin, and therefore it is a sin to remember a person who committed it. That's why you were trying to push her away from your memory. But in your heart you know this belief hurts you and doesn't let you mourn the way you want. Let it go now; realize it and let it go, because you need to learn other things. Sin, in the way your mind understands it, is a concept. Suicide is suffering. Don't judge it; help to transform the hurt it has left. So let go of your personal gaps to be ready to hear what I am about to say.

"I will need to tell you about sacrifice. A proper sacrifice requires the understanding of its proper time. This is very important, so please put all your attention into trying to understand this. The proper time is associated with the realization that death has happened. No one will ever escape the moment of realization of death after it comes. And it will come to you, you know. So you'd better be very attentive now to learn something that can help you then.

"As soon as one realizes that it is the experience of death one is facing, one has time to perform the ultimate sacrifice and free oneself completely from all fears. He needs to surrender everything in himself, everything from his former life, every single memory which would be otherwise indescribably dear to him at this crucial moment—surrender it to his *real* self, to the divine essence which has existed in his heart always and which is now ready to accept this ultimate offering.

"He needs to gather up his persona, his customs, worries, sadness, his desire to turn everything back and return to the world which is slipping away, and give everything he remembers about himself as a gift to the sweet and loving power concentrated in his heart. And the Great Mother who always lives in his heart because She gave him life will engulf him with Her loving presence, and he will be delivered from the fear of being inside death. She will continue his life forever if he remembers Her face and asks Her to save him. Lara hasn't completed this yet, but she still has the chance to do so.

"You have only a few hours left. Remember, there is responsibility in your path. So remain calm and keep moving."

I continue walking and soon I see the end of the forest, and the peak of a high mountain becomes visible. We—the dog, donkey, and I—get closer to the mountain, and I'm surprised to see many trucks driving along the roads on the mountain, as if they are carrying something out from the mountain. This image of the trucks is so astonishing that I stare at it for a while instead of moving forward.

Finally, I follow my animal and the obedient donkey with Lara's portrait. The mountain is treeless, covered by ancient white stones. It is so high and steep that it's hard for me to see its peak. I relieve the donkey of its burden and, without looking at it, place the portrait near one of the white stones. The donkey disappears without a trace. The small black animal is still near my feet, but I can predict it is not going to stay with me for long. When his eyes send me a good-bye sign, I know his departure is temporary, and that I will see the creature again sometime. Now I'm on my own again.

I hear a noise, as if an avalanche is forming on the mountain. A stream of sparkling light is coming down quickly from the mountain. As the stream of light flows to where the portrait stands, I know my task is to wait, be patient, and not interfere. The light envelops the frame and then freezes like a shiny ice around it, making a crystalline shield around the portrait. In seconds, the noise stops and everything returns to "normal," and the ice around the portrait is a miraculous mirror reflecting light.

The metal frame encased in the ice looks even bigger now. Suddenly, the two stones above the portrait move apart, making way for a yet more massive stone to appear in the space between them. It is the face of an old man. His eyes are shielded by gray lids. His motionless face shows wisdom and concentration. The face settles right above the frame. Pieces of ice start cracking. As if some powerful hand is breaking up the ice, it flakes off in splinters. The face slowly withdraws, the two stones move toward each other again, and the face is gone. What had been a rectangular metal frame is now transformed to more of an oval shape. Most of it is now dissolved. Then it all happens again. The stones part, giving way for the face to emerge. He directs his look again at the iced frame, and more pieces of ice are chopped away. So that shape now resembles a human. This process repeats itself five times.

Then the stone gates close and hide the face in the mountain. A slim young woman stands before me. Her body is still covered by a thin layer of shining ice, but it is so clear I can see details of her long white dress, the waves of her black hair combed back from her high forehead, her thin wrists and her white hands folded on her chest. I don't look at her face. I have to make myself turn away, for I know that I must not look at her. Under no condition can I meet her gaze or talk to her. It is difficult to turn away, for her presence is so alive.

I force myself not to remember even her name and keep myself turned away from her. Yet I feel her presence everywhere. The next moment I see her face, but it comes to me from memory, from one of those strange corners of the mind where you can find anything. She is a teenage girl in a white fur coat, leaning against a willow tree. She looks at the sky, swallowing bitter tears.

They flow abundantly from her wide-open eyes and rush down her cheeks, turning her face into a porcelain mask covered by thin, shining ice. It is Lara. She stands in our winter school yard. I remember she loved skiing, that she was the best in the class, always winning first place whatever distance she took. It was so easy for her, as if the skis were made with secret wings and she knew a way to make them fly. That day she was ready to become a winner. She took the skis like everybody else from the school depository and, putting on her ski shoes, walked out into the freezing air. It was a cold, shiny morning. The coach announced the distance to be skied and asked everybody to prepare and take their places on the track. She put her skis on first and moved easily toward a small hill of snow, not high, but still quite good to have fun riding down it. She stood on the top of this hill and, pushing her sticks strongly off the ground, skied off.

I didn't see how she fell. When I turned my head toward the hill, she was already on the ground, her white fluffy coat mixed with the snow so that at first glance it was difficult to separate them. Her blue knitted cap flew from her head, leaving her loose, black hair covered with snow. A piece of the broken ski stuck out from the ground, and the other ski had flown away from her foot to lie a few meters to one side.

I saw one of the worst boys in our class, the one who ended up in the jail for rape later in life, jumping in front of Lara, making fun of her tears. I saw her standing, snuggled up to the willow, with tearful eyes directed to the sky, trying to avoid his mockery. Was she crying because of pain? Were those tears of injury that her chance to win this main competition of the year was lost, for the coach didn't have time to replace her skis and just mumbled to her that she would get her good grade for the semester anyway? Or was it the boy that jumped around her?

I don't know why she cried. I wanted so much to come to her and say something warm and nice, but the minute I was going to make a step toward her, one of my other friends, Rita, ran up to me as if she felt my intention and raced me to the other side.

Rita was probably among those few people who for some reason disliked Lara. Rita herself was a very attractive girl, with swarthy skin, straight hair black as a raven's wing, and big, well-made-up brown eyes. Vital and mocking, she was a much more popular girl in our high school than Lara. She always tried to stand between me and Lara. "Gosh, she is so weak," Rita would say. "Do you know how easy it is for me to make her cry? You know it well yourself. I can't imagine how she is going to deal with it, when we are out of school. Pure hothouse plant, she created this artificial environment in our class, and it's okay with everybody. What is she going to do when we part? They are going to eat her alive and I think it's fair, for she always goes her own way instead of adjusting to other people. And you know, she can't be liked directly; she plays too lofty for that. I don't know why you choose to relate to her so kindly." That day Rita took me away from Lara, and from the other side of the field I saw Lara's figure standing by the willow with her head lifted up to the sky.

I see it again now. I know I can come closer to her and look at her and talk, for this is her image from my memory and I can allow myself to talk to the memory. I walk toward her through the field, seeing with my peripheral vision how Rita's surprised face fades away. I pick up Lara's blue cap from the ground, shaking the snow off it. I see how the boy's movements slow down with my every step, as if he feels me approaching from behind, without seeing me. I come closer to them and put my hand on the boy's shoulder. I know he remembers my anger well.

Once before he tried to mock me in front of my friends, testing the limits for future insults. He probably still remembers my face as I walked toward him, pushing him to the wall in the school hallway. He kept laughing and watching his friends behind me, expecting all of them to have a good laugh after this. I remember the sense of white rage that engulfed me as I pushed him toward the wall, the moment when my long, bright-red nails seized his thin neck and pierced his skin. His eyes widened and filled with horror as he realized that he couldn't talk or breathe.

I remember how my friends were trying to pull me away from him, but I kept squeezing his neck until I felt the mark I left on him would remain always and that he would never approach me again. Then I let my fingers go, and he continued looking at me with horror. When I turned to leave, I heard him saying to his friends, "She is crazy. Leave her alone."

I only had to turn and look back at him to make him say softly "sorry" and lower his eyes. He never bothered me again.

Now he turns to me after I touch his shoulder and his eyes fill with the same horror I saw in him in that school corridor. I see the mark on his skin my fingers left long ago and I know in one instant that I have power over him. His face shrinks into an apologetic grin; he tries to run away, to disappear, but I feel how my intention nails him to the spot, how his energy belongs to me. He says softly "sorry" with the same voice he did in the past.

I look straight into his light blue eyes, which are filled with fear. I feel this fear as a direct channel through which my will takes over his and he becomes susceptible to any transformation I may wish to cause in him. His eyes are fixed on me without blinking, as fear runs through his body, shaking it. After some time, I see how his eyes change and his body is totally transformed from man to wolf. There is no fear anymore in his wolf's eyes, only loyalty and obedience. I know that from now on he is ready to serve me. Only then do I let him go.

I hand the blue cap to Lara and say, "Larisa, don't cry, please."

She turns her big eyes toward me in surprise and stands motionless. The tears gradually disappear from her face. "You don't have to win this run. You are still the best skier without it. I know it's true." She smiles gently and nods her head a few times. I see how her face is changing and the desperate expression it had moments ago is fading away.

Her eyes brighten and she smiles, nodding her head again and again, as if she is ready to agree with everything I say. I feel that what is happening now changes my memory of her.

I feel Lara's presence, filled with her sorrows, her grief, her faith in sacrifice, and her hope and love. Memories circle her name, presenting everything and everybody in her consciousness. I know that the woman in a white dress released from the ice becomes one with the teenage girl from the school yard. I feel how, with every new memory, her sorrows and pain become keener, as do her love and hope.

Then I hear words spoken to her. It is a rather intent voice and it tells her, "The doors of your former house were hidden from you by foreign hands. Clasps on your clothes were buttoned up on the inside so that you couldn't unbutton them. And wind gathered and decided to destroy whatever had been planted. What is your problem still? Fear, careful and hiding itself deep in your family line, has been doing its business. Splash it out into the pail now, where everything foreign will be left.

"This is your past becoming the foreigner's present. You know your name again, and your name now takes on the form of a bird. Restore your speech, and leave the silence with the former shape. You still see what it is to be darkened. You still take on the weight which was long since abandoned, and again and again you strive to die, going from yesterday into tomorrow. Only then will you fly to another space, when yesterday and tomorrow are dead for you, and when weight and expectation are dead for you. With their departure, the sun will lift you up higher and higher. Farther away and less dangerous, the door will be left for you, behind which a greedy second death hides itself, waiting for you. Lie to it, give it your clothes, throw your rings and bracelets into its face along with your fondest desires; give them up, and give up your death, for the former world has passed away."

Lara turns around and pushes her ski sticks firmly off the snow, and her skis take her quickly toward the white, sunlit space held open for her. She skis so well. It is her best run ever and she doesn't have anything in her way to stop or hurt her. She goes straight toward the immense sun disk, which holds her gently in its rays. I know that my task is accomplished. I know that Lara now is in a place from where she can move on freely and nothing will stop her. I see the horizon lit with the sun and feel strongly that somewhere near it, there is a space for me, too. I feel its presence strongly, as if I had experienced it before in a few rare moments of childhood when the world seemed to be made of light and there was no fear.

Seeing this fills my heart and sets it vibrating, and Michael's hand moves softly off my shoulder again and I see the face of the God of Time, looking straight into my heart, the same way I saw it in the tent in Afrasiab a few days ago.

The fire flames pulsate in the middle of the ground and Sulema's kind face, that reminds me of my grandmother's face so much, now moves slightly to another side of the fire. I understand that the fire and the sun are extensions of my heart and that this is a true territory of the God of Time. It is her territory. The Great Mother lives here, inside the sun, and it is her love that unites all separated memories. She has the power to forgive everything, for she gave life to everything. She fills in all space with her acceptance, and she doesn't allow fear or guilt to exist in her territory. She deletes fear and guilt as separated memories which reproduce the hurt, and she makes life whole again. The world belongs to her again as at the very beginning, and life continues by her will.

For the first time, I realize that God is not a mental concept but an alive, powerful, vibrating being and we all belong to Her. The understanding comes to me. I know that Lara found her way to the Mother when her receding figure merges with the sun disk and it accepts her fully and my memory of her becomes healed and complete.

The other memory knots connected to it become untied and I see Varvara, the girl from the hospital, with her reddish eyes and attacking smile, coming indecisively closer to the fire in the center of Sulema's yard. Its warmth touches her and she can finally return to herself, to the little girl who was hurt undeservedly and who cried silently in her family's backyard behind the tall green bush until sundown.

The Sun fire touches the scars on Varvara's wrists and smoothes them away as it smoothes away her harshness and anxiety. She finally feels so unconditionally protected that she allows herself to become gentle again. Next, I remember Masha and she stands right near me now, full of wonder, open, but still hesitant to believe in herself.

I experience these memories almost at the same time, and the change that this experience causes in me produces a realization of the main memory gap I carry in myself. The gap that everybody of my time carries, the biggest gap in our memory which creates the biggest fear: the fear that we forgot the face of the Mother, that we forgot Her name.

This realization fills my memory and everything painful in it becomes protected and transformed. A sweet sensation fills my heart with gratitude and I want to give all these memories to Her, the Great Mother who always loves and always forgives.

I feel such gratitude toward Michael for facilitating this experience for me. Thinking of him focuses my perception on the fire. I see Sulema's attentive face on the other side of the fire. The moment my eyes meet hers, she stands up and walks to me, bearing a cup of water. I drink the cold water. It firms my perception of the moment and I come back to myself fully, sitting on the ground in her backyard, carrying deep in my memory all the healing changes that came to me from the fire.

Somehow I know without looking that Michael has left and I won't see him. I don't feel sad about it because I understand it was supposed to happen this way. He knows better and I trust him and his way. I don't say anything to Sulema, but nod my head in thanks. My mouth is still dry and somewhat bitter and my body is very relaxed. She takes Michael's *chetki* off her wrist and puts it around my neck. The beads are so light and feel warm under my fingers as if they took a little of the Sun fire into themselves.

I look around and see the grass. I smell its freshness. I hear the rustling of the bushes. My senses feel clear and unbiased as I remember them from childhood. There is no boundary between me and life. I have nothing to prove, nothing to fear. I only have to be and belong.

Sulema takes up the cups from the ground. We shake the blanket out and take it inside. Sulema is silent and the only thing she says to me before we leave is this, "He went back to his island where he lives most of the time. At least I think so. He didn't say. Or he may have gone to the mountains to see his Gypsy grandfather. In any case, I'll be waiting for him to come back."

After that, she takes me back to the bazaar by the same road we came in by when I met her and Michael in the morning.

Chapter 15

Back at the bazaar, Sulema hugged me just like my grandmother would. Then she left, saying she needed to buy vegetables and that since the prices at the end of the bazaar day should be good, she was in a hurry.

I stood there, without moving for a while, in the middle of the bazaar square near the Bibi Khanum mosque. The colors, human voices, laughter, arguments, the smell of fat burning on the ancient open stoves mixed with the spicy aroma of endless herbs brought from all over to the Samarkand bazaar—all were a tremendous magnet holding and facilitating my new awareness. I thought again how wise Sulema was to take me to the bazaar before sending me back to the hotel.

I heard a tambourine played nearby. I saw a large peacock proudly making its steps on the ground among the group of men who were trading it. The bird almost danced to the sound of the tambourine as if it were preparing itself to become a decoration of somebody's hidden palace.

One of the men surrounding the peacock left the group and walked toward me, smiling confidently. He looked like a middle-aged Uzbek, with short dark hair, dark pants, and silk shirt unbuttoned at the top. Only after he made a few steps toward me did I realize it was Vladimir.

There had been so many things I thought I would ask him those first days in Uzbekistan when I still hoped to find him. Now I was simply glad to see him and there were no questions I wanted to ask.

He greeted me kindly and then asked me to return his *chetki*, since it was time for me to leave and it needed to stay in Samarkand. I touched the warm beads and held them for a moment before giving them back to Vladimir, who wound the *chetki* around his right wrist.

He walked me to the hotel and told me he had just returned from Novosibirsk. He said that Victor and Phil might be flying to Samarkand next month. He also said that Masha wouldn't come, at least for now, for she had sustained a serious nervous breakdown.

"She had to be hospitalized. I don't know the details, except that she requested to come to your hospital and be treated by you. So she is waiting for you. When you return home, treat her well."

"I will." I knew I would.

After giving me this news, he walked in silence for a while and then said, "I know, Olga, that sooner or later you will raise a question to yourself. The same question your Western culture carries with it through ages. Was it real or not? Was it subjective or objective? Let me tell you what we think here about this question. Consider it the end of my lecture, to which I didn't give closure."

He smiled and talked while we walked from the bazaar to the hotel. He spoke with a lecturing tone in his voice, but it didn't irritate me, because I felt that his only intention was to convey the knowledge to me. I perceived him already as a man of great knowledge and I wanted to hear what he had to say.

"The only real difference between what is called subjective and objective experience is defined by the position of attention. Common people still make a huge difference between inner and outer experiences, and they tend to consider as 'objective' only the outer events. It happens because the attention of these people has not been trained to focus on interior reality, including dreams.

"A child develops only those patterns of attention which are supported by the majority. People learn throughout their life how to join their attention with other people's attentions to see reality the same way everyone does. When they go to sleep and enter the dream state at night, they are left alone, and unless they have been through special training, their dream attention is weak. The experience is less tangible, because less attention is put into generating it. They call it subjective and not real.

"So if only you were told that other people had seen the same images you had, experienced the same reality, you would breathe a sigh of relief and would start considering your own experience as more objective. It takes a lot of power to learn for yourself that the significance of reality and experience doesn't depend on other people supporting it, but is connected with the experience's ability to touch and activate the deepest patterns of transformation in you.

"You can make your internal experiences, first of all your dreams, 'objective' by practicing the focusing of your single attention on them, and thus freeing yourself from the imposed collective streams of interpretation.

"I know that you understand what I am saying not only intellectually, but on a deeper level where you can always feel and recognize the presence of the truth. Samarkand has accumulated great awareness in dream reality through the efforts of many people working here from generation to generation. It makes everything you have experienced here real and objective. You have now become part of the work that has been done here for the ages, and it will be your job now to make this work known to more people in your world. I know you have all the abilities to be successful in accomplishing this task. You are firmly grounded in both realities. You have had other significant experiences before, and you have a respect for the tradition.

"Plus, there are more important tasks for you in the future, but your success with them will largely depend on how you are able to translate what you have learned here in Samarkand to other people who need to learn about it. Your major obstacle can be your doubt. Remember what I said and don't let the spirits of trauma poison you with their doubts, and don't change the memory of what happened to you here.

"We are the dream healers. The connection between dream healers around the world now needs to be reestablished. The dream healers exist not only in Uzbekistan, but in other places on Earth. They have been connected mostly through the dream tribe that wanders between remote lands, between past and present, between here and beyond. I know you saw some of the people from this dream tribe, the *liuli*, the Central Asian Gypsies."

His last phrase makes me stop. I look at him and some loose ends connect.

"You know Michael, don't you?"

He looks at me silently and smiles warmly, a smile that reminds me of our first meeting in Novosibirsk. "Of course I know him. What did you think? I invited you here."

His smile is so disarming and clarifying that it dissolves all my questions, for somehow through his smile I understand everything that I need to know. The only question I have left to him is the question about Michael.

"Vladimir, do you think I will be able to see him again?"

"Michael is a very special man. He has an unusual life. You can't predict him. He lives his life differently from many people. And he lives inside of dreams as well. He is the master of lucid dreams and there, inside your dreams, you can always find him, whenever you need to." After saying that, Vladimir added with laughter, "And even though you didn't ask it, yes, you will be able to see me again. I will return to Novosibirsk in a few months. I like people in your city."

A few hours later, a taxi driver took me to the airport. When we were driving near Afrasiab with the chain of Shakh-i-Zendeh mosques stretched along it, the driver turned to me and said, "We call this place the place of the Alive King. I can tell you why he is still alive. Or maybe you know it already?"

"Thank you. I do."

Chapter 16

On one of the days when I was with Michael in Samarkand, Masha was about to turn the key to open her apartment door in Novosibirsk when loud screams and the sound of someone being hit commanded her attention. She took a few steps down and saw a group of men dressed in black surrounding a young man at his apartment entrance. The man had been Masha's neighbor for a long time. She knew him quite well, even though their acquaintance had never gone beyond a standard neighborly "hi." He was thin, of short stature, and he never looked one straight in the eyes, as if he was afraid of something. Even now as he tried to resist the force of a few well-built men, one of whom was already locking handcuffs around his wrists, his attempts to fight were so nervous and weak that he looked pathetic.

"What are you doing?" Masha screamed, not thinking about the consequences of her interference. The men in black civilian suits could have been part of a criminal gang but she didn't care about her safety. She just felt the need to protect her neighbor.

"All is fine, relax," the oldest man in the group said to her while his fellows were pushing the neighbor toward the stairs and he continued to resist.

"We are a special force group. This is all legal. Don't worry. And be grateful that this son of a bitch is out of your house, so you can sleep easily."

"What did he do?" Masha almost whispered the question, for everything inside of her feared hearing the answer.

But the man heard her and before going downstairs with his group toward two black cars, he took a moment and, looking straight into Masha's eyes, told her, "Finally, it's over. He was the last one of the three of them who tortured the entire city for so long. You have heard, of course, the horror stories about disappearing women in the city. Everybody knows about that. These fucking monsters kidnapped the girls, kept them hostages in a house outside the city, raped and tortured them, and then killed them all. One of the girls pretended to die and they buried her in the forest. But she was alive and she escaped. She led us to the group. We took the two others already. He was the last one. He is a medical student, believe it or not. He can start praying to his god now to get capital punishment. He doesn't want to know what would become of him in prison should they let him live. But it's over now. You can sleep easily, sister."

The man left, but from that exact moment Masha was unable to sleep. She started drinking heavily the same day, and was on a drinking bout for three days, still unable to sleep, when her grandmother found her in the apartment. Masha was running around her room, which was trashed this time more than ever. She hadn't eaten or slept all this time and she hadn't been answering the phone. She was so agitated that it was impossible to have a conversation

with her. She kept pacing around, ignoring her grandmother, who called the ambulance right away. The only
phrase that Masha kept saying, alternating whispers with
wild screams, was, "He was living in my house." The
phrase didn't make sense to anybody and Masha was
admitted to my hospital with an initial diagnosis of alcohol psychosis.

I read part of this story in her chart the first day I came
back to work. The rest of the story I learned from Masha
later. I read it sitting in my office while Masha was sitting
in the chair in front of me, in exactly the same place where
she had sat at our first meeting. She refused to talk to anyone in the hospital and refused to see any visitors, including Smirnov, who, as I knew from the staff, tried to
contact her every day. She was taking her medications
without problems and looked somnolent. She was very
calm—a stony calm. Her face without makeup was very
young and pale.

She didn't look at me, but I had a sense that our connection wasn't altered by her mental condition. I still had
a strong feeling of being connected with her and that connection felt even stronger now.

"You probably are too tired to talk now, Masha. I think
it may be better if I tell you first what happened to me in
Samarkand since you didn't have a chance to go with me.
It may be helpful for you to hear it. Are you interested?"

She looked at me for the first time and said in a soft
voice, "Of course, I am interested. I didn't really have a
chance to go with you."

I saw the trace of relief in her face when she realized
that I wasn't angry with her for not going to Samarkand.
Through that relief I also saw how much guilt and shame
she still carried in her.

"Before I tell you about my journey, I want to tell you,
Masha, that one of the main things I learned there is that
we are not guilty for the hurt that other people have caused

in us. It is not our fault that we got hurt and it's not us who should be ashamed of it."

She looked at me with heightened attention and didn't say a word, but I saw that she heard my words and that on some level she accepted the message they carried. When I told Vladimir that I would heal her, I didn't know exactly how I would do it. I didn't prepare any plan. But I felt that my intention to heal was greatly supported now by Michael's lessons and by my experiences in Samarkand. All that told me that telling Masha the story of my journey in Samarkand would be the best form to convey healing to her. So I did.

I chose to use my experience as a therapeutic story. I told it to Masha step by step, guiding her through all the moments of my time in Samarkand, through all the details and nuances of my experiences. I reconstructed that space for her, carefully choosing my words and using them consciously as a verbal bridge to guide her from despair to the place where she could find the healing she needed. Her natural ability to go into trance was now reinforced by the effects of medication. She soon forgot her surroundings and sat in front of me with her eyes wide open, motionless and enchanted. Her enlarged pupils pulsated slightly every time she heard something significant, and she would nod her head.

She listened to my story as if she were watching a movie, and her state influenced me to the point that, at one moment, I almost saw Michael standing in front of me, behind Masha, his hand on her left shoulder and smiling to me. He was almost real, his presence was so strong. Then, at the moment when I was about to finish my story, I imagined Michael's hand moving lightly off Masha's shoulder and at that very moment she shook her head and woke up from her trance enchantment. Now she was sitting in the chair in front of me, awake, concentrated and serious, and looking impatient to tell me something.

"You need to let me go home *now*," she said, as if it was a matter of life or death. She didn't comment on my story. She looked so occupied with something this story had created in her that implementing it was the only thing that mattered for her at that moment.

"Okay. But what's the rush? Why does it have to be now and not tomorrow or in two days?"

"I can't tell you that. I have to go home. I have to be alone. I need to take a shower and to do some other things. You don't get a decent shower in this place. And I haven't eaten decent food here for a few days already. I need to do my stuff and I will be back tonight."

I remained silent and kept looking at her. She was agitated by some idea and she didn't want to tell me about it. She was brought to the hospital in restraints a few days ago and she still remained very unstable in her impulses. To let her go home was a very tough choice, and I was reluctant to make it.

Understanding my doubts, she looked at me and said, "I have never been suicidal. You don't have to be afraid of that." Then she got silent, waiting for me to reply.

I felt Michael's presence in the room again. I could sense him laughing, and it showed me clearly that all my doubts were my own fears from the past and that they had nothing to do with Masha and her situation, and that going home was exactly the right thing for Masha to do. I breathed in relief and smiled to her.

"Okay. Go home and take a shower. I hope you can tell me about your idea sometime soon. Be back at eight."

"I will. To make it easier for you, I will ask Smirnov to go with me. He's been waiting here since this morning."

"I don't know if it makes it easier for me, but if you want to go home with him, it's your decision."

Masha left. I saw her, through the window, getting into Smirnov's black car. I saw Smirnov helping her to get in, suddenly looking older and helpless and at the same time happy that she had finally agreed to see him, and I was surprised to see how much he cared about her and how much he was hurt by her recent breakdown.

My day went by quickly. I was busy after my days of absence from work and I didn't think about Masha. Only when the nurse stopped in my office before leaving home and asked me if I would ever leave tonight, did I realize that I was waiting for Masha to come back, and that I would stay until she did. I didn't feel worried about her at all, but I wanted to see her back in the hospital.

Exactly at eight o'clock a white taxi stopped behind my window in front of the ward entrance. Smirnov got out first and opened the back door for Masha.

I stood up from my chair and walked toward the window to see her better. She was dressed in a white spring coat that contrasted with the long black hair flowing over her shoulders. The sky was so gray that I had completely forgotten it was the middle of spring already. Now Masha's image with her white coat, her careful steps through the melting snow on the ground, acutely reminded me of spring. She looked like a manifestation of spring itself, so alive and beautiful, so full of energy.

She saw me behind the window and waved to me cheerfully. Smirnov stayed outside in the waiting room as she walked straight into my office and took a seat on the same chair as before. She looked different. Her gaze was direct and open, and she was shining.

"Thank you for waiting for me. You probably are tired after such a long day," she said with concern in her voice, and that was different, too. Not because she didn't care about other people before, but because being preoccupied with her own matters, she simply didn't have enough energy in the past to notice how other people felt. She had much more energy now and it was radiating from her.

"I see that you look quite different, Masha. What did you do that changed you so much?"

"I did what you taught me to do," she answered with a smile on her face.

I didn't interrupt her and waited for her to continue.

"I did a ritual. Indirectly, you taught me to do it. You didn't give me any suggestions, but your intention to help and the story you told me created a clear understanding in me of what I had to do to heal myself. When you were talking about your memories and about your friend, I knew exactly what she was going through. I knew the pain and shame of being violated. But in her case it was one isolated event that shook her reality and she killed herself trying to kill that memory. In my case, to kill myself would be the easiest choice and I would have done it long ago if my memory and my shame were not incorporated so much into who I was.

"I grew up being sexually abused by my uncle, who had been raping me since I was seven years old. It was at that age that my parents went to work abroad and left me with my father's brother. They couldn't take me with them—at least that was what they told me. I guess to leave a child was a warranty to the state that they wouldn't defect.

"When I was ten, they came to visit here for one month and it was awkward. My mother was very beautiful, nice, and totally distant. Or maybe she pretended to be. I didn't feel her as my mother anymore, not the way I remembered her. My father was irritated with everything, including me. I guess we didn't come up to the standards of the quality of life he had in the West, and he felt embarrassed to have to confront his Russian past. He was very proud to have lived in the West, and considered himself a man of another class. They brought me a lot of stuff—jeans, a tape recorder, cosmetics. I didn't use cosmetics then, and I was embarrassed to ask my mom how to use them. Every time she looked at me and said, 'Masha, you are so pretty,' I wanted to run away and never show my face to anyone again.

"I saw my uncle's face as he was looking at my mother at those moments, and it was so scary. I saw how attracted he was to her and how much hatred and jealousy he had toward my father. And I knew at age ten that they would leave again soon and he would come to my bedroom at night to not only physically rape me but, through me, degrade my father and get at my mother. I didn't tell them about it at their first visit.

"At age fifteen, I had my first boyfriend, Sergey, who had to make me almost unconsciously drunk before I would sleep with him for the first time. He liked it. I used him to get rid of my uncle's night visits. I told my uncle that if he ever entered my room again, Sergey would kill him. He believed me, I guess, and called me a 'fucking bitch.' But he didn't send me away. He wanted the money and all the stuff that my parents sent regularly from abroad. By social standards, we were very rich and many kids at school told me how lucky I was to have exchanged my parents for all the goods that I had. I left my uncle's house on the day when I turned eighteen.

"The next day I called my parents, who were working in Spain at that time, and told them about everything. My mother flew back and placed me in a hotel. She was so concerned about the damage that my story could cause to their public image that she chose not to believe me. She was very polite and distant again, and she kept saying that whatever happened, it had happened already, and now we needed to think about my current disposition. She used that exact term 'disposition' as if I was an object that needed to be placed in the most secure environment in order not to cause any troubles.

"I didn't hate her. I think it was around that time that I found it entertaining to watch people's behavior from outside and not to react to it. My mother was the first one I observed this way, and I simply didn't like her. But I also saw how easy it was to manipulate people, so I started to do it regularly. My mother soon went back to Spain, but before she left, she 'disposed' me to live with my grandmother, the one you talked to on the phone the other day. She was always living here in Novosibirsk, but I never knew her before. She wasn't technically my grandmother because she was the mother of my dad's first wife, who drank herself to death. I didn't have any clue that my father was married before, but I learned a great deal about his first wife after her mother agreed to take care of me. She exchanged her two-bedroom apartment in the city for two small apartments and we lived close to one another since then.

"She showed me pictures of her daughter and told me stories about her. She never blamed my dad for her daughter's drinking and death, but I knew that she was thinking the same thing I was thinking—that my father was a pig and that he was guilty of destroying that woman. He had never talked to me again since he learned about the sexual abuse. He erased me from his life because now I wasn't simply irritating but also dangerous, dangerous to his sense of power and security. He would never admit that his younger brother could have gotten to him that much. He sent me only a car—a red Jeep for my twentieth birthday—and that was it.

"I never had any hope for my future. I never felt that I had a future, really. Never until today, when I heard your story. It revealed to me a dimension within myself that I never knew existed. When you talked about the Great Mother, I had a sense that it was my real mother you were talking about, not biologically, not as a replacement for the mother I lacked in my life, but as a mother who actually gave me life by Her will, and I felt hope for the first time. I felt such a connection with Her. I realized at some point in your story that the fact that I was alive and breathing was an exact manifestation of this connection, and that only through it could I heal myself. I left home feeling so dirty from all the shame I had experienced in life, but I also felt that I was ready to be cleansed from it and that the Mother would help me to do that.

"But I needed a shower or bath. When we came to my apartment, I asked Smirnov to wait in the kitchen, and he did. He was very nice and quiet the whole day today. I went to the bathroom and filled the bath without having any idea what I would do, just following the call to be cleansed. Leaving my clothes on the bathroom floor, I sank into the warm water and floated for some time. I don't know how long I stayed there. I felt sad but peaceful. And then I started to cry. I wasn't sobbing; tears just rolled down my cheeks. I tried to smile and not to feel sad, but the sadness was too great to avoid.

"I remembered what you told me, that when we feel sad we believe that we are guilty of something. I realized that all these years I had carried with me the belief that everything happened to me because I was such a bad person, and if I were a better girl, my parents would never leave me and nobody would ever hurt me. I realized that it was not true, that it wasn't my fault that I got hurt, and that there was no reason for me to be ashamed. Then, in my heart, I called to the Mother and asked Her to heal me from this hurt and to take it away.

"The water was so still. I couldn't even feel my breathing. I think I was in some sort of trance, but it wasn't as scary as before. Every time before, I would go into trance and see my uncle approaching me and my parents watching him from outside, laughing. This time it was very still. There was nobody but me in the water.

"Then suddenly it was almost as if the ceiling above me parted and the sky behind it approached me, carrying a live, beautiful red flower and somebody's invisible hand was giving it to me. The flower was vibrating and turning, and when it came closer I saw that it was a spinning swastika approaching me.

"I felt scared for a second, because I have been afraid of swastikas from childhood. I have Jewish blood, and I think my blood froze at that moment. But then I remembered what Michael told you about this image and my fear dissolved. The swastika kept turning and approached my chest. It entered my body through my chest and I felt unspeakable joy in my heart. I closed my eyes and I didn't think of anything anymore. I knew that it was the power that would cleanse me from inside.

"Smirnov taught me some techniques to work with abuse issues, but it was always on the surface. Those techniques never changed anything in my internal space, and that space felt filthy to me. I never used birth control because I thought I was infertile. At that moment, I realized that I wouldn't get pregnant because I couldn't allow my body to accept a child into a space inside that was contaminated by my uncle's flesh. His cells were still somewhere inside me. Parts of his flesh continued to poison me, and I realized that I was unconsciously waiting for cancer or something like that to help me to get rid of my female organs. The swastika was turning inside my body from my head down to my chest and farther down, cleaning every cell of my body. The substance of the water was like a mother's hands that held me softly and protected me from screaming out loud from all the pain in my past that became so evident to me. I lay in the water still and tried not to move.

"Then I experienced a strong blow inside, down in my abdomen. I felt almost torn apart from inside. I screamed loudly because it was such an intense pain, and with my scream the swastika ran down my uterus and exploded out of my body into the water, taking with it everything that didn't belong to me. The images of my uncle, mother, and father left me with it and dissolved in the water.

"I laughed when Smirnov knocked on the bathroom door. I felt so happy. I told him that I would be out in a minute and asked him to put on some tea. I stood up in the bath and turned on the shower. The water was streaming down my body and I felt so fresh and beautiful, as if I was an ancient goddess just born from the water.

"It was a very simple and quiet feeling. It wasn't ecstasy or elation. It was a down-to-earth understanding that finally it was over for me, and that now I could start to live my own life. The sense of my future became tremendous. It was as if a whole universe became open for me. Everything became so clear. I was clean.

"I went to the kitchen and had some tea with Smirnov. He didn't ask me anything, but I saw in his eyes that he was happy to see how I had changed. He asked me to forgive him but didn't say what for. I said I forgave him and then I talked to him about practical details. I asked him to find me a good buyer for the Jeep, and he has already made a phone call. I will probably sell it tomorrow. It will give me enough money to travel abroad. You know, before today I promised myself I would never leave this country and never would go to the places where my parents were. I will do it now. I am ready to go out into the world and to claim it for myself. It belongs to me as much as to anyone else. So I will live in it. I think I will go to Spain first."

I walked Masha to the waiting room. Smirnov got up from the chair and greeted me almost formally. I was surprised again to see the transformation in this man. His irony, his mental tricks, were gone without a trace and he was very serious. He looked as though he finally had found something that had an immense value for him. I knew that it was Masha and her well-being, but I didn't sense any romantic involvement. He was treating her like a daughter who had just recovered from a grave disease. He looked as though his recent experience had made him reconsider many things about himself that he had thought were solid and absolute. He looked happier and much more real. He looked very strong and powerful now, in this new state.

He thanked me, shook my hand, and walked Masha outside. Before leaving, she turned to me and waved again and asked in a cheerful tone, "I am officially discharged from here, right?"

When I silently nodded my head, smiling, she said, "Thank you, doctor," and they left.

It was time for me to leave, too. I was about to open the door when it shot open and two orderlies walked inside, accompanying a thin woman in a hospital gown who walked with small steps as if trying to postpone the inevitable—being checked in to a psychiatric unit. As I waited in the corridor for them to pass by, she lifted her head and I recognized her in a moment. It was Katherine, the woman I had admitted before going to Samarkand. Apparently, she was coming back, after being discharged not long ago, and she didn't look well. She recognized me, but she didn't say a word. She looked away and her face became tense.

"Hello, Katherine," I said as gently as I could, and she said a soft "Hello" back to me, still looking away.

"I will be your doctor now, Katherine. It is too late today. I have to go home. But tomorrow I will come back in the morning and we will talk. Try to have a good night. I will see you tomorrow."

She looked at me and nodded her head. I moved aside, allowing her and the orderlies to pass by. The door to the ward closed behind them. I stood in the corridor for a while, trying to put my thoughts and feelings together. I didn't feel confused or anxious anymore. And I didn't feel powerless anymore either. I felt that there was a lot of work to do ahead of me. And I liked that feeling.

Index

About the Author

Olga Kharitidi, M.D., author of *Entering the Circle: Ancient Secrets of Siberian Wisdom Discovered by a Russian Psychiatrist* (HarperSanFrancisco, 1997), was born in Siberia. She received her medical training in Novosibirsk and worked as a psychiatrist in the former Soviet Union. Dr. Kharitidi spent much time studying ancient traditions of Siberia and Central Asia; as a result of her travel and study, she developed a new system of healing psychological traumas. Dr. Kharitidi is a practicing psychiatrist in the United States and teaches workshops and lectures on the "transformation of trauma" throughout the world. She lives in Minneapolis, Minnesota.

Hampton Roads Publishing Company
. . . for the evolving human spirit

HAMPTON ROADS PUBLISHING COMPANY
publishes books on a variety of subjects,
including spirituality, health, and other
related topics.

For a copy of our latest trade catalog,
call 978-465-0504 or
visit our website at www.hrpub.com